Forgiveness

*To Kim,
Forgiven,
Roland and Hayes Taylor*

Forgiveness

The Key to Lasting Joy

ROLAND & GAYLE TAYLOR

WinePressPublishing
Great Books, Defined.

© 2013 by Roland and Gayle Taylor. All rights reserved.

WinePress Publishing is honored to present this title in partnership with the author. The views expressed or implied in this work are those of the author. WinePress provides our imprint seal representing design excellence, creative content and high quality production. To learn more about Responsible Publishing™ visit www.winepresspublishing.com.

No part of this publication may be reproduced, stored in a retrieval system, or transmitted in any way by any means—electronic, mechanical, photocopy, recording, or otherwise—without the prior permission of the copyright holder, except as provided by USA copyright law.

Unless otherwise noted, all Scriptures are taken from the *New King James Version*. Copyright © 1982 by Thomas Nelson, Inc. Used by permission. All rights reserved.

Scripture references marked KJV are taken from the *King James Version* of the Bible.

Scripture references marked NASB are taken from the *New American Standard Bible*, © 1960, 1963, 1968, 1971, 1972, 1973, 1975, 1977 by The Lockman Foundation. Used by permission.

Scripture references marked TLB are taken from *The Living Bible*, © 1971 owned by assignment by Illinois Regional Bank N.A. (as trustee). Used by permission of Tyndale House Publishers, Inc., Wheaton, Illinois 60189. All rights reserved.

Scripture references marked NLT are taken from the *Holy Bible, New Living Translation*, copyright © 1996, 2004, 2007 by Tyndale House Foundation. Used by permission of Tyndale House Publishers, Inc., Carol Stream, Illinois 60188. All rights reserved.

Scripture references marked NIV are taken from the *Holy Bible, New International Version*®, *NIV*®. Copyright © 1973, 1978, 1984 by Biblica, Inc.™ Used by permission of Zondervan. All rights reserved worldwide. www.zondervan.com

ISBN 13: 978-1-4141-2391-2
ISBN 10: 1-4141-2391-4
Library of Congress Catalog Card Number: 2012910385

Contents

Authors' Note vii

1. Forgiveness: The Key to Happiness in Marriage 1
2. Forgiveness: The Key to a Happy Family 23
3. Forgiveness: The Key to Harmony in the Church 53
4. Forgiveness: The Key to Surviving Tragedy 75
5. Forgiveness: The Key to Heaven 97

How You Can Experience God's Forgiveness 115

About the Authors 117

Notes 119

Authors' Note

WHY WOULD A couple of senior citizens feel compelled to write a book about forgiveness? Because over the years we've seen devastation in lives when individuals reject God's forgiveness and refuse to forgive each other. By contrast, we've seen the miraculous transformation that forgiveness brings. Life is all about forgiveness—receiving God's forgiveness and extending it to others.

Our insights come from our perspectives as a minister and a teacher in addition to our roles as parents and grandparents. We write about what we've heard, seen, and experienced in our own family, our church family, and in the life journeys of our friends as well as those we've only read about.

The motivation for writing this book is our desire to help people experience God's forgiveness through Jesus Christ and learn to forgive.

If you haven't received God's gift of forgiveness through Christ, we invite you to do that now. If you don't know how you can be sure God has forgiven you, please turn to the end of this book and read "How You Can Experience God's Forgiveness."

Forgiveness: The Key to Lasting Joy

The Christian's mission is to tell people that God loves them and wants to forgive their sins. Life, now and eternal, is all about forgiveness. Receiving forgiveness and extending it to others is the key to lasting joy.

—Roland and Gayle Taylor

1

Forgiveness: The Key to Happiness in Marriage

*U*NTIL DEATH US do part.

Has it ever crossed your mind that your marriage is killing you and you want out? You may think your marriage isn't *that* bad, but you realize it isn't as good as it once was.

Peter Marshall, two-term chaplain of the U.S. Senate, called marriage "the halls of highest human happiness." Forgiveness is the key to that happiness we all seek in marriage.

When a man and a woman come together and promise before God that they will love, honor, and cherish each other as long as they live, and they keep that promise, marriage truly does become their highest human happiness. Conversely, when two people break their promise to each other and to God, marriage can become the halls of highest human misery.

We know from Scripture that God blesses marriage. It is so important that the Bible compares it to God and His people and to Christ and His church. All who receive God's forgiveness through Christ are a part of the church, which is called the bride of Christ.

My husband and I have truly had "the halls of highest human happiness" marriage. God had special plans for Roland and me, as He does for all of us. It was by obedience to those divergent plans that our lives converged at Twentynine Palms, California.

Forgiveness: The Key to Lasting Joy

After I completed my BA degree, I enrolled at Whittier College for postgraduate studies, but two weeks later my dad asked me if I would come home and manage the ice cream parlor where I had worked from my early childhood. To love and honor my parents, and to follow what I felt was God's will for me, I went home.

It was a little lonely living in the homestead house by myself because when I was growing up there it had been bursting at the seams with six children. By this time, most of my friends had moved away, and my parents and my younger brother and sister had gone to Arizona for rest and recuperation. I didn't have time for a social life anyway because our business was open from eleven a.m. to eleven p.m., and after closing I often made ice cream until two a.m. Don't get me wrong. I may have been tired at times, but I knew I was in the place where God wanted me, and it really was a great experience to operate a successful business. I may not have been the foreign missionary I'd hoped to be, but I had been called to my own mission field behind the counter. I had great opportunities to share my faith with my customers.

I was in many weddings in college and I knew it had been said of me, "Always a bridesmaid, never a bride." I had romantic dreams of falling in love with Mr. Right, who of course would be a dedicated Christian. He might even be a Rev. Right, and we would serve the Lord together.

In the meantime, a young man of great character and talent had dedicated his life to serving the Lord. He was preparing for ministry at California Baptist Seminary. Roland put himself through the Bible Institute of Los Angeles and California Baptist College by selling Bibles, vacuums, and sewing machines from door to door. He continued as a door-to-door salesman throughout seminary. With work, and his desire to maintain the highest grade point average, he had very little time for dating. He knew that in God's good time he would find the girl God had kept just for him.

In his final year of seminary, Roland was assigned to assist in the preaching and teaching ministry at a church in Twentynine Palms. A boy in his Sunday school class told him about a Christian girl who would be a perfect match for him. It was inevitable that

Forgiveness: The Key to Happiness in Marriage

Roland would go to the popular ice cream parlor at Smith's Ranch, and it was there over a delicious ice cream soda that he met me, his future wife.

Roland and I were married in the Little Church of the Desert on May 5, 1956. The *Desert Trail* newspaper wrote:

> The wedding of Gayle Smith and Rev. Roland Taylor was probably one of the greatest events in Twentynine Palms history. As a wedding it was a gorgeous display of the beauty and sanctity of the most sacred of all relationships. It was one of those weddings where "God joined together," and where dignity and plain common sense dominated; no man will ever "put it asunder."

If you are single and think it's time to get married, but the right one hasn't burst onto your matrimonial screen, don't get impatient and settle for Mister or Miss Wrong. Wait and continue to pray for the one God has for you in His perfect timing. Many people get ahead of God and come to the point in life where they say, "If I'd only waited. If only I hadn't married...." You don't want that to happen to you. God's timing is perfect.

One of our greatest joys is that our children have wonderful spouses to whom they have remained happily married. Our older son has celebrated twenty-six wedding anniversaries, our second son, twenty-five, and our daughter, fifteen. Each anniversary is a celebration of God's goodness in bringing these special couples together. Roland officiated at the wedding of each of our children.

Long before each child met the one he or she would marry, Roland and I prayed that God would keep them and their future life's mate committed to Christ and to following His standards. We asked God to keep each of them for the person of His choosing.

Our conviction was that whom our children married was of far greater importance than even the choice of their life's career, as significant as that is. The first most important decision in life is to commit to follow Jesus Christ as Savior and Lord. The second most important decision is the choice of whom you will marry.

Forgiveness: The Key to Lasting Joy

Roland and I both knew that we could only marry someone who was a Christian. Scripture tells us: "Don't team up with those who are unbelievers" (2 Cor. 6:14 NLT). There is no closer team than that of husband and wife.

As a young man, Roland traveled as a soloist with a well-known evangelist. This wise man gave him many pearls of good advice. Chaplain Anderson said, "Never date a girl you know you wouldn't want to marry." Following that admonition prevented him a lot of hard feelings and potential misery, to say nothing of the financial drain it saved on his limited resources.

Our emphasis in this book is primarily on forgiveness, not marriage counseling; however, a lot less forgiveness will be needed and there will be fewer painful arguments for which forgiveness is required if you marry the right person. This doesn't mean your mate will be perfect, and certainly, you won't be either. Love doesn't mean you'll never have to say, "I'm sorry." But in all probability you'll have to say it less often if you and your spouse have compatible goals and convictions. The question comes to us: "Can two walk together, except they be agreed?" (Amos 3:3 KJV).

There are certain important issues that need to be agreed upon before a couple becomes too serious about spending their life together. Faith and family should be prominent in planning for a future as husband and wife. How many children you hope to have, where you would choose to live, and the way you view finances should be compatible. You certainly will want to agree on your choice of a church home.

When Roland and I became engaged, we talked and planned for our own Christian home. We wanted to have children and train them in the love and fear of God. We knew we would read the Word together. We would give a tithe of our income to the Lord, and we would serve Him with gladness.

There are many misunderstandings that can be avoided if agreement is reached on these big issues of life before marriage. Of course you will have disagreements—you can't resolve every potential problem before it arises. You are individuals with many years of differing interests. The kind of music you enjoy, the kind

Forgiveness: The Key to Happiness in Marriage

of food you prefer, and the sports you like may not be the same. Your differences may be part of the reason you were attracted to each other.

When major purchases you make or vacation destinations become an issue, try to be considerate of the other person's reasons for an expressed preference. You can come to an agreement, but it often will require that each of you gives a little or sometimes gives a lot. Let's remember the good advice, "... in honor giving preference to one another" (Rom. 12:10). You'll be surprised how happy it will make you to give in to the preferences of the one you love.

When Roland and I moved into a new home after we retired, he let me have free rein over decorating the house. He didn't quibble over cost (of course I'm very thrifty, and he appreciates that fact). He knew he would have input because I always value his opinion and approval.

When it came to landscaping our backyard, Roland wanted a cascading fountain. I thought the bank where it was to be installed was too steep and that a fountain would require too much upkeep. I saw the problems; Roland saw the beauty. Without making a big fuss, I deferred to his wishes. We now have a lovely fountain, which is a source of continuing pleasure as we listen to the music of the splashing water and watch the hummingbirds drink and bathe. I often thank Roland for his good-natured stubbornness. The fountain has added a wonderful touch to the enjoyment of our home.

The words came to me again, "Be kindly affectionate one to another with brotherly [wifely] love, in honor giving preference to one another" (Rom. 12:10).

We remember our wedding as a harmonious occasion. The groom's brother arrived a little late and postponed the ceremony a few minutes. An uncle on the bride's side of the family became overly zealous with the rice and we found it in our gifts and clothing for months, but nothing could tarnish the luster of our special day.

Forgiveness: The Key to Lasting Joy

As pastor of a youthful congregation, Roland performed lots of weddings. Congregations often fall into one of two categories: elderly or youthful. The first requires many funerals, and the second is blessed with many weddings. Christ's love and the love of bride and groom for each other and for the Lord were preeminent in each ceremony Roland conducted.

Your minister may have said something like the following in your wedding ceremony:

> The ring is made of gold, that metal which is least tarnished of all metals. It is circular in shape, indicating that it has no ending, signifying the permanence of the vows that are sincerely made. The ring is given in token and in pledge of your constant affection and abiding love.

The ring's message is the permanence of the marriage covenant. We are to remain true to the promise made to God and to our mate.

Not all weddings retain the occasion's solemnity. Roland's first wedding was made memorable by the bride's uncontrolled hysterical laughter. This lovely girl continued to laugh throughout the entire ceremony. Despite her hilarity, she was able to affirm her love for her groom, and to Roland's relief the service came to a successful conclusion. To the best of our knowledge the couple has remained faithful to each other.

Roland has always quoted 1 Corinthians 13 in his wedding ceremonies. This beautiful treatise on love is very meaningful in the King James Version of the Bible, but it is also helpful when read from a modern translation such as the New Living Translation:

> If I could speak all the languages of earth and of angels but didn't love others, I would only be a noisy gong or a clanging cymbal. If I had the gift of prophecy, and if I understood all of God's secret plans and possessed all knowledge, and if I had such faith that I could move mountains, but didn't love others, I would be nothing. If I gave everything I have to the poor and even sacrificed my body, I could boast about it; but if I didn't love others, I would have gained nothing. Love is patient and kind. Love is not jealous

Forgiveness: The Key to Happiness in Marriage

or boastful or proud or rude. It does not demand its own way. It is not irritable, and it keeps no record of being wronged. It does not rejoice about injustice but rejoices whenever the truth wins out. Love never gives up, never loses faith, is always hopeful, and endures through every circumstance. Prophecy and speaking in unknown languages and special knowledge will become useless. But love will last forever! Now our knowledge is partial and incomplete, and even the gift of prophecy reveals only part of the whole picture! But when full understanding comes, these partial things will become useless. When I was a child, I spoke and thought and reasoned as a child. But when I grew up, I put away childish things. Now we see things imperfectly, like puzzling reflections in a mirror, but then we will see everything with perfect clarity. All that I know now is partial and incomplete, but then I will know everything completely, just as God now knows me completely. Three things will last forever—faith, hope, and love—and the greatest of these is love.
—1 Corinthians 13:1–13 (NLT)

Although this entire chapter in 1 Corinthians is of great value and can speak to our hearts without interpretation, let's focus on what love is and then make the contrast to what love is not.

What love is:

- Love is patient.
- Love is kind.
- Love never gives up.
- Love never loses faith.
- Love is always hopeful.
- Love rejoices whenever the truth wins out.
- Love will last forever.

What love is not:

- Love is not jealous.
- Love is not boastful.
- Love is not proud.

Forgiveness: The Key to Lasting Joy

- Love is not rude.
- Love does not demand its own way.
- Love is not irritable.
- Love keeps no record of when it has been wronged.
- Love is never glad about injustice.

Love looks for the good. It requires that we express appreciation to God and to our spouse. We should have thanksgiving in our hearts and on our lips every day. It's too easy to see others' faults and the problems around us if we don't realize that the eyes of love look for the good in people and circumstances.

When I look at my home I can see dusting to be done, windows to be washed, and showers to be scrubbed, or I can see a cozy hideaway with books, pictures, and comfortable furniture. It's all in how I choose to look at it. I like to say that I don't wear my glasses to clean house because I see too much dust.

When I walk in my yard I can see beautiful flowers or I can see ugly weeds. The flowers are there and the weeds are there. What do I look for? Unless I'm looking for a good weed-pulling workout, I choose to focus on the flowers.

I don't want to wear my critical glasses when I look at my husband, and I certainly don't want him to wear his when he looks at me. I'm sure I look much more attractive in candlelight or moonlight than in a spotlight or magnifying glasses.

> Finally, brethren, whatever is true, whatever is honorable, whatever is right, whatever is pure, whatever is lovely, whatever is of good repute, if there is any excellence and if anything worthy of praise, let your mind dwell on these things.
> —Philippians 4:8 NASB

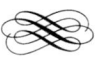

Kindness is a vital key to a lasting marriage. Kindness is the key to keeping your husband. Kindness is the key to keeping your wife. Let's spend some time focusing on kindness before we address the forgiveness needed when you fail to be kind.

Forgiveness: The Key to Happiness in Marriage

I have at various times felt the urge to add my drop in the bucket to the volume of marital advice that is flooding today's market. Unfortunately, much that is being written is not to anoint marriage with the oil of kindness but rather to rub it with the crude oil of self-gratification.

There's a simple little key hidden away in Proverbs 31:26 that can unlock the door to your husband's heart, ladies. It is the key of kindness. In the Living Bible, it reads, "Kindness is the rule for everything she says." When kindness becomes the rule or law for everything we say, our marriage will be transformed.

My mother, and probably yours too, always said, "Think before you speak" and "if you can't say something good about a person, don't say anything at all." Most of us never stop to think that maybe this includes what we say to or about our spouse.

The book of Proverbs reminds us that "it is better to live in the corner of the roof than in a house shared with a contentious woman" (25:24 NASB), "it is better to live in a desert land, than with a contentious and vexing woman" (21:19 NASB), and "better is a dry morsel and quietness with it than a house full of feasting with strife" (17:1 NASB).

These verses all seem to tell us that regardless of where you live or what you eat, you won't be happy without kindness in your home.

We need a kindness key. When it is misplaced, we should search diligently until we recover it. Then remember: a sincere apology with a request for forgiveness will restore harmony in the home. We should try to keep our kindness key with us at all times. When we lose it we need to ask forgiveness.

Husbands also need to remember that kindness is the key to a happy home. Your kind, thoughtful comments to your wife might even make her a better cook and housekeeper. They could also motivate her to become more glamorous and affectionate. You can't lose. Kindness brings very positive results and it goes a long way in promoting a happy marriage.

Husbands and wives, let's pray the prayer in Psalm 141:3 (KJV): "Set a watch, O Lord, before my mouth; keep the door of my lips."

Forgiveness: The Key to Lasting Joy

We need to think before we speak. Remember that "a gentle answer turns away wrath, but harsh words stir up anger" (Prov. 15:1 NLT). How obvious it is that kind, soft words calm anger. We are admonished to "be kind to one another, tenderhearted, forgiving each other, just as God in Christ also has forgiven you" (Eph. 4:32 NASB).

After we retired, we took a trip to China. There were twenty-eight people in our tour group from all over the United States. Although we had been married for more than forty years, some of our traveling companions were convinced we were newlyweds. We may have held hands and chosen to sit with each other, but we certainly were not overly affectionate in public. In trying to analyze why they thought we were recently married, we came up with only one logical answer: we treated each other with kindness and respect.

We've noticed that some couples belittle each other (often unintentionally). Sometimes a spouse tells a joke at the other's expense. This often comes off as ridicule, causing hurt feelings, resentment, and discouragement. We need to build up each other's sense of worth and self-esteem, not tear it down.

We cringe every time we hear a radio commercial featuring a prominent talk show host in our area. In promoting a hair restoration system, he says his wife has used this product to keep her hair beautiful. He says, "She has beautiful hair, but everybody knows the rest of her is a mess." We know this is meant to be a joke, but it's a prime example of a hurtful joke.

I don't know any wives who take kindly to their husbands' jokes about their hair, weight, cooking, or housekeeping. Roland doesn't know any husbands who appreciate their wives joking about their weight, strength, or golf scores either.

It doesn't make one appear smart or clever to tell a joke at his or her mate's expense. Instead, it makes them seem mean and inconsiderate of the other's feelings. Inconsiderate teasing often requires an apology to repair the damage caused by thoughtless and hurtful humor.

Forgiveness: The Key to Happiness in Marriage

And now we come to the subject of nagging, on which I am an expert. Sometimes I feel a little grouchy for no reason. Maybe I hear something on the news or experience a little annoyance, and my usual positive thinking becomes negative and I turn into a nagging wife. When I feel a bit grumpy and want to take it out on my husband, this verse hits me on the head: "It is better to live alone in the corner of an attic than with a contentious wife in a lovely home" (Prov. 21:9 NLT).

I always like to keep our home as beautiful as finances will permit, but the beauty I enjoy becomes unattractive even to me when an ugly atmosphere of strife creeps in. I tell myself to snap out of it, and I ask God to give me a thankful heart.

The verse, "A nagging wife annoys like a constant dripping" (Prov. 19:13 NLT) speaks loudly to me because nagging is one area where I sometimes exceed the bounds of a loving wife and become that constant dripping. At such times I don't think Roland wants to hear me say, "I love you." I think he'd much rather hear me say, "I'm sorry," or say nothing at all.

Is there any excuse for nagging? I like to think there are two areas in which nagging is a virtue because they are both prompted by love. I am a backseat driver; my mother was, and I am. I backseat drive because I love my husband and I don't want to get us killed. Another excuse is that we live in Southern California and drive the freeways.

The second thing I nag about (out of love, of course) is what my husband eats. I'm especially judgmental when we go out for breakfast and he orders bacon. Once again, my motive is pure because it comes from my love for him. I want him to eat healthfully and live a long life. But I think he'd gladly give up a year or two of life if I'd be quiet and let him enjoy his bacon! We've solved this problem—we just don't go out to breakfast anymore.

As you look at the wedding ring on your finger, you are reminded of that special day when you exchanged rings with the one you

Forgiveness: The Key to Lasting Joy

married. Although your ring may be very beautiful and valuable, its real value is not its purchase price; rather, it is the symbolic meaning of the golden band you wear. The ring's message is the permanence of the promises you made on your wedding day. You pledged to be true to each other in sickness and in health, in joy and in sorrow.

Marriage is a wonderful relationship that God has ordained for humankind's happiness. It is a joyful experience to be married to the right person, but there will be times of sickness and sorrow when matrimony's ties are tested. During these difficult times, couples need to cling closely to each other and to God.

There can also be danger in good times. Sometimes affluence and success pose a greater challenge to a marriage than hard times do, because when we feel too self-sufficient we often fail to rely on God and each other.

There may come a time when your emotional attraction to each other is diminished. One partner can become disillusioned and desire to return to the freedom of single life. He or she may be tempted to disregard your marriage vows. It is at such times that couples should read a good book dealing with the subject of faithfulness in marriage, seek counseling, or attend a marriage enrichment seminar. Emotions may fluctuate, but the commitment you made to God cannot be subject to your feelings.

We have known and counseled couples that were at the very brink of divorce. Sometimes the husband and sometimes the wife would say, "I just don't love [her/him] anymore." When they were willing to be reminded of the promises they had made to God and to each other, some of them chose to work to save their marriage. With God's help and with prayerful resolve, the seemingly impossible becomes possible. We've known many couples who have gone through contentious times but have chosen to work out their differences and have stayed together.

Marriage is like a tree buffeted by the wind. It can sink down deep roots and become stronger because of the tempest. When the quarrels of the past are forgiven and there is a mutual desire for reconciliation, love can grow and flourish again.

Forgiveness: The Key to Happiness in Marriage

God honors those who keep their promises and remain married, even when well-meaning friends or divorce lawyers suggest an "easy" way out. He rewards a faithful couple with a loving and happy marriage that can last a lifetime.

Do you feel you and your spouse are drifting apart? If so, you may be trying to ignore that nagging thought, but little things keep you wondering if your love is a thing of the past. Take action—don't let your love wither and die like some neglected vine. Love needs to be cultivated and nourished. Maybe it's time to review what love is and what love is not. Read, study, pray, and obey the message found in the "love chapter," 1 Corinthians 13.

Perhaps you've heard of best-selling author Janette Oke's book *Love Comes Softly*, which was also made into a Hallmark film. Love does come softly sometimes, and it also returns softly to a broken relationship when there is forgiveness.

If your marriage hasn't been the "halls of highest human happiness" experience, it can be, starting today. It doesn't matter if you've been married one year or fifty years. Ask for forgiveness and begin again. It all starts with you. You'll be amazed at how your partner will respond. A long and happy married life is all about forgiveness.

A delightful elderly couple came for lunch every week to Carol's Kitchen, where we serve lunch to disadvantaged people. They were absent for a few weeks and then their granddaughter brought her grandmother, but the grandfather was missing.

I asked, "Where's your husband?"

She replied, "He fell and broke his hip, and he's in a nursing home."

Weeks passed before both of them finally came back to lunch. They were radiantly happy, together again, after an unfortunate separation. The bride of seventy-two years patted her groom's hand and said, "He's the best man there is."

There's lots of good advice to be gained from couples that have lived happily together for many years. The book *Married for Life:*

Forgiveness: The Key to Lasting Joy

Secrets from Those Married 50 Years or More by Bill Morelan contains what he calls "inspiration from those married fifty years or more."

The most frequent tidbit of advice seasoned married couples share is, "Don't let the sun go down on your anger." That means you shouldn't go to bed angry or even leave your home angry. Ask for forgiveness, kiss, and make up. You'll have a more peaceful night's sleep or a better day at work.

I've known many thoughtful, caring people, especially my mother, but I've never known anyone who didn't need to apologize to someone at some time in his or her life. It doesn't take an intentional act of meanness or cruelty to hurt someone. Neglect or lack of attention can wound. Never having to say, "I'm sorry" is a myth. Never saying, "I'm sorry" is a mistake—a very big mistake.

We often hurt those we love the most. A careless word, an insensitive joke, or a sarcastic remark can hurt someone deeply. At such times love doesn't mean we never have to say, "I'm sorry." Real love can't wait to say, "I'm sorry." It is also true that real love can't wait to accept an apology.

God wants us to ask for His forgiveness and He will freely give it. Our spouse wants to know that when he or she asks for forgiveness we will give it unconditionally. We might want to get historical and rehash old issues, but God doesn't do that to us. When He forgives, He forgets. We should too.

We should enter into marriage with the heartset and mindset that it is a lifetime commitment, but every couple will experience times of testing. At such times a sincere apology and a recommitment to God and to each other becomes essential. When we do this, we will not need to ask for forgiveness as often because we will be sincerely putting God and our spouse first in our lives.

We've heard people say, "I'll never forgive him/her for that." It's almost said with pride, as though there is virtue in such resolve. There are times when we just don't feel like forgiving. We don't want to apologize. We think that the situation will get better by itself. There are also times when we get a strange pleasure by letting the storm brew and sulking over our real or imaginary hurt. But God doesn't view an unforgiving attitude as a virtue.

Forgiveness: The Key to Happiness in Marriage

Sometimes you may think that you're always the one who has to apologize—your spouse never apologizes. That may be true, but isn't it worth it to you to be the peacemaker? Remember: "Blessed are the peacemakers" (Matt. 5:9 NASB). If you do your part by sincerely apologizing and even going the extra mile in trying to restore peace to your home, that's all you can do. Ask God to do the rest.

We all want security: financial security, job security, and security in marriage. Gary Smalley has written many volumes containing wise marriage counseling. In his book *I Promise: How 5 Commitments Determine the Destiny of Your Marriage*, he points to security as the most important ingredient in a couple's relationship.

So which comes first: security or forgiveness? There will be no security if there is no forgiveness. Part of being secure is the assurance that you can ask for forgiveness when you fail and know that God and your partner will forgive you. Even in a couple's dating and engagement days there are times when asking for forgiveness is necessary.

When you find something very annoying about your spouse, take a look at yourself. It is most likely you have a corresponding problem with your own behavior and attitude. "Why do you look at the speck that is in your brother's [husband's or wife's] eye, but do not notice the log that is in your own eye? Or how can you say to your brother, 'Let me take the speck out of your eye,' and behold, the log is in your own eye?" (Matt. 7:3-4 NASB). Watch that judgmental attitude!

Basically we are all self-centered and self-righteous. We make excuses for our own failings (if we even admit we have any) and we accuse our partner. It's so easy to see someone else's faults and be blind to our own. Correcting others' faults is not our responsibility. Correcting our own faults and becoming more Christlike is what God requires of us.

Most often if we change our own offensive behavior it will lead to a corresponding change in our spouse. Paul admonishes us to "get rid of all bitterness, rage, anger, harsh words, and slander, as well as all types of malicious behavior" (Eph. 4:31 NLT). We need

Forgiveness: The Key to Lasting Joy

to delete these attitudes just as we delete any undesirable material that appears on our computer screen.

But it isn't enough just to get rid of the undesirable aspects of our lives. We also need to emphasize the positive virtues. In the words of an old popular song, "You've got to accentuate the positive, eliminate the negative; and latch on to the affirmative; don't mess with Mr. In-between." Paul puts it this way: "Be kind to each other, tenderhearted, forgiving one another, just as God through Christ has forgiven you" (Eph. 4:32 NLT).

The book *The Power of Positive Thinking* by Norman Vincent Peale has had a big influence on my life. There is power in positive thinking—power to change attitudes and relationships as we make the choice to think the best about people. Positive thinking leads to positive living.

The power of positive living is demonstrated in kindness. Kindness changes people. It changes relationships and attitudes. Kindness between a husband and wife speaks louder than outward displays of affection. Kindness speaks even louder than the words, "I love you."

The power of forgiveness is even stronger than our good thoughts and actions are. Forgiveness can pick up the broken pieces of life when we fail to think and live as we know we should. Forgiveness can rebuild homes, hearts, and dreams.

It's obvious that major issues need to be forgiven and forgotten, but sometimes a minor incident that should have been resolved the day it happened lasts a lifetime. We heard of one well-meaning new husband who brought home a bouquet of carnations for his wife. Instead of accepting them graciously, she said, "Thank you, but I like roses better."

Her husband was hurt and angry and said, "I'll never bring you flowers again."

That was some twenty years ago, and he has never presented her another bouquet.

Forgiveness: The Key to Happiness in Marriage

When kindness becomes the casualty of anger, we need the power of forgiveness. When your spouse hurts your feelings, count to ten, breathe a prayer, and remember that "a gentle answer turns away wrath, but a harsh word stirs up anger" (Prov. 15:1 NASB).

When we forgive and we sense we are forgiven, the sun is brighter, the sky is bluer, and the grass is greener. God puts a song in our hearts. Extending and receiving forgiveness lightens our steps and boosts our spirits. Being forgiven and receiving forgiveness lifts a weight (like losing a hundred pounds) and gives us new energy for life.

Many people waste too much time and energy lamenting over what they have or haven't done. They blame themselves for investments they've made or failed to make. Sometimes they go so far as to bemoan, for example, that "great-grandfather sold his property at Hollywood and Vine." They are convinced they would be rich if he only had used better judgment.

Those people are like the football player who berates himself for years because he missed a field goal that would have given his team a victory. Whether a professional athlete, a child playing Little League baseball, or a senior citizen on the golf course, we shouldn't let our successes or failures determine how we feel about ourselves. We usually learn more from our failures than from our successes anyway.

Michael Jordan, considered one of the greatest basketball players of all time, lost three hundred games and missed twenty-six times when he was given the ball to make the game-winning shot. Jordan attributes his success to how he used his failures as motivation to succeed.

In any avenue of life we are bound to make blunders. Our mistakes can have a devastating effect on our life or our failures can become stepping-stones to success. What should we do when we are depressed over our failures? Sometimes we need to ask God to forgive us. We may need to seek forgiveness from another person.

Forgiveness: The Key to Lasting Joy

However, it is also important for us to learn to forgive ourselves. Failure to forgive ourselves is in reality a denial of the completeness of the forgiveness we have asked God to grant.

We've all read about or seen on TV stories of teenagers, or even adults, who have done something foolish and in their shame have seen no way out but suicide. How tragic that they didn't know that the way forward was to receive God's forgiveness as the reason to forgive themselves.

The apostle Paul could have spent his life regretting his atrocities against the followers of Christ when he was the early church's chief persecutor, but he found a way to overcome: "Forgetting the past and looking forward to what lies ahead, I strain to reach the end of the race and receive the prize for which God is calling us up to Heaven because of what Christ Jesus did for us" (Phil. 3:13 TLB).

God has forgiven me and I've forgiven myself, but I must remember that I'm a work in progress. I will fail again, but God isn't finished with me yet. With God's help, I choose—for my own well-being and happiness, and for the well-being of those around me—to accept Christ's forgiveness, forgive myself, forget the past, and move forward.

A few years ago I was reminded of the need to forgive myself. It was our son and daughter-in-law's twentieth wedding anniversary and we were entrusted with the care of our dear granddaughter they adopted from Uganda.

Reluctant to leave their daughter for a short trip, the conscientious new parents prepared in detail for her every need and desire. Each morning at breakfast, Sarah would find a love note from her parents with clues for a treasure hunt. She searched the house until she was rewarded with a special treat or toy.

One day Sarah bubbled with excitement because she was going to go swimming at her day camp. We hurried to finish breakfast and help Sarah with her treasure map. In no time she found a little chest described in her note. She lifted the lid and took out a ring with a big jewel that looked like a real diamond. With a squeal of delight and a big smile, she put it on her finger and danced around the house.

Forgiveness: The Key to Happiness in Marriage

We grabbed her backpack and jumped in the car, hoping to arrive at church in time for her to catch the bus for her ride to day camp.

That afternoon when she got off the bus, Sarah wasn't quite her exuberant self. She explained that when she was swimming, her ring had fallen off her finger and sunk to the bottom of the lake. She said she and her friend kept diving to find it, but it was lost in the mud.

We tried to comfort her and told her it wasn't her fault. We assured her that her mom and dad could buy her another ring. I thought if I knew where I could find a dollar store, I would replace it myself.

That night I had a frightful thought that maybe, just maybe, the ring Sarah found in the jewelry box wasn't a fake diamond. Maybe it was the beautiful solitaire engagement ring our son had given his bride-to-be some twenty years ago. I tried to put the ridiculous thought out of my mind.

When our son and daughter-in-law returned from their anniversary trip, they were greeted by their healthy, happy girl who was delighted to see them and by her tired, but proud, grandparents who felt they had done an admirable job of babysitting.

With trepidation I broached the story of the ring. To my horror I found that indeed I had not known the difference between a little girl's toy ring and an expensive diamond made priceless by its sentimental value. I had let my granddaughter swim with her mother's diamond on her finger.

Our children never spoke to me of their disappointment over my ignorance. They never showed any anger or shed any tears over the loss of the ring. Their concern was to comfort and encourage me. They forgave me immediately. It took a little longer for me to forgive myself.

My children taught me a lesson on forgiveness. Now I understand that even a cherished and valuable diamond engagement ring is, after all, only a trinket in time.

Whether you're lamenting over a lost trinket or even a lost treasure, forgive yourself and move forward. You'll be miserable and you will make those around you miserable if you don't forgive yourself. It isn't pleasant to live with someone who continues to be tortured by past mistakes.

In today's world it seems impossible to write about marriage without referring to the subject of divorce. The Bible discourages divorce and in some cases prohibits it. However, God meets us where we are and offers forgiveness and new life.

There are countless famous people whose stories of infidelity have been emblazoned across the TV screen. We are saddened when we hear that those whom we have admired are involved in scandalous affairs. We are sorry for the embarrassment and hurt they've caused their families. We are also concerned about the degrading influence their behavior and public disgrace have on society.

We've all known friends or family members whose seemingly happy homes have been blindsided by an unfaithful spouse. Not only is the couple's life shattered, but there are also serious consequences in their children's lives for years to come.

Many of the offenses that culminate in divorce seem outside the possibility of forgiveness. In cases of unfaithfulness to the marriage vows, there is so much hurt, anger, and distrust that the partner who is wronged feels it is impossible to forgive. God doesn't wink at infidelity, but He does forgive the truly repentant sinner.

David, who was a man after God's own heart, committed the sin of adultery and tried to hide it with the sin of murder. He knew that all sin is sin against God. When the prophet Nathan confronted David with his sin, he repented and confessed his sin to God. When David experienced God's forgiveness, he wrote: "Oh, what joy for those whose disobedience is forgiven, whose sin is put out of sight! Yes, what joy for those whose record the LORD has cleared of guilt, whose lives are lived in complete honesty!" (Ps. 32:1–2 NLT).

Regardless of the magnitude of the moral infraction of unfaithfulness, no situation is ever made better by withholding forgiveness. The hurt spouse doesn't deny the other's wrongdoing by forgiving.

Forgiveness: The Key to Happiness in Marriage

In addition to spurring personal healing, forgiveness must be offered for the children's sake. Many times children end up taking the adult's place and being the arbitrators and peacemakers between their parents. It isn't fair for children to be caught in the middle of visitation and custody battles.

If you are the injured party in a bitter divorce and are disillusioned with your mate, or if you are overwhelmed with your own guilt over the breakup of your marriage, take your hurt to God. Ask for His forgiveness and pray sincerely that He will help you to forgive your estranged spouse or forgive yourself. Then, as difficult as it may be, offer forgiveness and/or let him or her know that you hope forgiveness will be offered to you. When you accept God's forgiveness, and forgive yourself, you've done all you can do. It's a brand-new day and you have a new life to live.

Many divorces are the result of insignificant disagreements that are allowed to fester and grow from the proverbial molehill into a mountain that becomes insurmountable. Couples need to settle their disputes promptly with a sincere apology and forgiveness. Forgiveness is the key to a lasting marriage.

Our fifty-fourth wedding anniversary was the most turbulent day of our long and happy marriage. We're glad to report that the disturbance wasn't between us, but with the Pacific Ocean's angry winds and waves.

We were celebrating on a four-day cruise from San Diego to Vancouver when a fierce storm whipped the waves into billowing whitecaps. The groom enjoyed a lavish anniversary dinner while his bride languished in their cabin with seasickness. When the storm passed, the sunrise seemed more brilliant and the sea more placid than ever before.

This is true in a storm on the ocean or a storm in a marriage. When the tempest has passed and calm takes the place of turmoil, we have a new appreciation for the blessings of life. What does it mean to be married fifty-four years? Certainly it means we're old.

Forgiveness: The Key to Lasting Joy

We also like to think it means we've experienced a lot of life and hopefully learned a little from life's lessons along the way. We've had a full and happy life. It isn't because we've done everything right—far from it.

We believe our marriage has been happy because we both received God's forgiveness through Christ in our youth and we've learned to forgive each other. Life has been and continues to be all about forgiveness.

Your Turn

1. How do my spouse and I usually handle situations where we ought to apologize?

2. What are some tangible things I can do to help restore trust and harmony in my marriage?

3. Am I willing to forgive past grievances and trust God to help me forget them?

2

Forgiveness: The Key to a Happy Family

A PSYCHOLOGIST WROTE A book titled *Rules for Raising Children*. Several years passed and he married and became the father of toddlers. His publisher called him and said that they wanted to release a second edition of his book and asked if he wanted to make any changes.

"Only one," he said. "Change the title to *Theories About Raising Children*."

The years passed and the author's children grew to be teenagers. His publisher contacted him and said the book had sold so well that they would like to publish a third edition. They asked if he had any corrections or changes.

"Only one," he said. "Change the title to *Myths About Raising Children*."

How-to books and magazine articles provide a wealth of information on everything imaginable, from losing weight to becoming a millionaire. In the olden days, Dr. Spock was considered to be the expert on the subject of raising children, but we preferred to follow the Bible and Dr. James Dobson's Christian advice from his ministry, Focus on the Family. There are lots of myths about raising children, but the Bible is the source of the tried and true pearls of

Forgiveness: The Key to Lasting Joy

wisdom on the subject. Those who follow God's plan will have the one dependable source of guidance.

We need a blueprint to build a house, a recipe to bake a cake, and rules to play a game. Far more important than any of these is our need for a guide to raising children. We need the biblical plan to build a Christian home where the lessons of faith, kindness, forgiveness, love, and all Christian virtues are taught by word and example.

The apostle Paul thought of Timothy as his young son in the faith, but he recognized the importance of Timothy's home schooling. The faith of Timothy's mother, Eunice, and his grandmother, Lois, who instructed him in the holy Scriptures from his early childhood, were a great influence on his life. Paul wrote to Timothy:

> You know how, when you were a small child, you were taught the holy Scriptures; and it is these that make you wise to accept God's salvation by trusting in Christ Jesus. The whole Bible was given to us by inspiration from God and is useful to teach us what is true and to make us realize what is wrong in our lives; it straightens us out and helps us do what is right.
> —2 Timothy 3:15–16 TLB

In Timothy's home and in our homes today, it is the teaching of the holy Scriptures that brings our children to salvation in Jesus Christ and teaches them what is right and wrong. Children need to receive God's forgiveness through Christ and learn how to forgive others.

Years ago we attended a conference where C. Oscar Johnson, the famous pastor of Third Baptist Church in St. Louis, Missouri, was the featured speaker. He said, "My father was a blacksmith. He didn't use store-bought horseshoes; instead, he would throw a strip of iron into the fire, and when it was white-hot he would use a pair of tongs to hold it against the anvil and by tapping it with his hammer he shaped it to fit the individual horse. My job was to pump the bellows to make the iron hot. One day when business was slow, I asked him if I could make a shoe. He seemed amused, as he replied, 'All right, I'll pump the bellows and you make the

Forgiveness: The Key to a Happy Family

shoe.' I did everything I had seen my father do, and when the iron was white-hot, I used the tongs to hold it against the anvil, and I began to tap it with the hammer. The more I tapped, the stranger it looked, until my father picked it up with a pair of tongs and, holding it in view, he said, 'Son, I've never seen the horse that could wear this shoe.' When he saw how chagrined I was, he smiled and said, 'Let's make one together.'"

Dr. Johnson went on to emphasize the importance of working with our heavenly Father as we endeavor to shape our children's lives. Any attempt at doing the job in our own wisdom is inadequate, he said. We must depend on God's guidance through the Bible and through earnest prayer.

May your prayer be, "Dear God, please let's do this together. We know we need Your help in raising our children."

We are instructed in Deuteronomy 6:6–7, "And these words which I command you today shall be in your heart. You shall teach them diligently to your children, and shall talk of them when you sit in your house, when you walk by the way, when you lie down, and when you rise up."

Your children need to know that you believe what the Bible tells us. One of the first songs we taught our children was, "The B-I-B-L-E; yes, that's the book for me. I stand alone on the Word of God, the B-I-B-L-E." As toddlers, they sang that song and "Jesus Loves Me" at the tops of their lungs.

We need to impress on our children the importance of obedience to God's commands. You can do that by your own obedience to the Bible's teachings. We go to church because God tells us to. We give to the poor because God tells us to. We obey our parents because God tells us to. Obedience to God should be illustrated in everything we do.

Dr. Peter Marshall had a favorite story. A little boy in Scotland was generally very obedient, but on one occasion his mother served a bowl of prunes at the end of the meal. The little fellow disliked

Forgiveness: The Key to Lasting Joy

the prunes, so he ate all except three before he announced that he was not going to eat the rest. His mother insisted that he eat them all, but those three prunes remained as a symbol of his stubborn disobedience. His mother begged and threatened to no avail until she said, "God will be angry with you if you don't obey your mother." When he remained defiant, she told him to go to bed. No sooner had he followed her instructions than a terrible storm erupted. The lightning and thunder shook the house so violently that the mother became concerned about her boy. She pictured him cowering in his bed in terror, so she crept upstairs and opened the door a crack just in time to see him standing by the window, looking out at the storm. She heard him mutter, "My, oh my, such a fuss over three little prunes."

God requires that children obey their parents, not just because mommy and daddy tell them to, but even more importantly because God tells us in the Bible, "Children, obey your parents" (Eph. 6:1). A child should be encouraged to memorize the fifth commandment: "Honor your father and your mother, as the LORD your God has commanded you, that your days may be long, and that it may be well with you in the land which the LORD your God is giving you" (Deut. 5:16).

The apostle Paul writes in Ephesians, "Children, obey your parents in the Lord, for this is right. 'Honor your father and mother,' which is the first commandment with promise: 'that it may be well with you and that you may live long on the earth'" (Eph. 6:1-3).

The Christian life requires self-discipline. It is often said, "Judge me by what I say, not by what I do." The ideal is to speak what is right and then follow it up with right action. Sometimes our actions are a direct contradiction between what we say and what we want to teach our children.

God, in His great love for man, said to Moses, "Oh, that they had such a heart in them that they would fear Me and always keep all My commandments, that it might be well with them and with their children forever!" (Deut. 5:29). God promises that it will go well with us and with our children if we are obedient to Him.

Forgiveness: The Key to a Happy Family

Of course you want your children to have a long, happy life. God promises that the way to do this is for children to obey Him and to obey their parents. You do your children a great disservice if you do not teach them the fifth commandment with its beautiful promise. Children need to understand at an early age that there are consequences to disobedience. Their choices and actions will affect the length and quality of their life. You need wisdom in striking a happy balance when you teach them the fear of God and the love of God.

God's love assures us that forgiveness is available. Children must know that there is a way to restore fellowship with their earthly parents and with God. As parents, there will be times when you fail to obey God's commandments and there will be times when your children fail to obey you. Children need to know that they can ask and receive forgiveness from God and from their parents. Ask God for forgiveness.

There's a story about an English mother who lost her only son in World War I. Nothing could release her from her deep depression. Day after day she mourned her loss until one night she had a dream. An angel appeared and told her that she could have her son back for ten minutes. "What time in his life do you want him brought back to you? Would you choose when he was an infant, cradled in your arms? Would you want him back when he was a little boy, going off to school for the first time? Would you prefer to have him return to you dressed in his military uniform, just before he went marching off to war?"

The grieving mother hesitated for a time before she replied, "No, not at any of those times. I want him back at the time when he was a little boy. I had refused to grant one of his requests and he begged me to change my mind, but in spite of his pleading I remained firm in my decision. He broke into tears and shouted, 'I hate you! I hate you! I don't like you anymore and I'm going away and I'm never coming back to you.' In a fit of anger he stormed out into the garden.

"Some time later he came back. With tears coursing down his little cheeks, he held out his arms to me and asked me to forgive

Forgiveness: The Key to Lasting Joy

him. 'I've been a bad boy and I'm sorry, Muvver. Please forgive me. I won't be bad again, and I want you to hug me.'"

The heartbroken mother looked up at the angel and said, "That was the time I loved him the most. Oh, angel, give me back my boy when he cried tears of repentance and when he longed for my forgiveness and my love."

Jesus told the beautiful parable of the prodigal son to illustrate the depth of God's love for every sinner who repents and asks for forgiveness. God's arms are always open to receive the repentant one who comes to Him through Jesus Christ, His Son. Let's remember that all of life, including family life, is about forgiveness. God gives us a warning and a promise to help us raise children. The warning is "Discipline your children while there is hope. Otherwise you will ruin their lives" (Prov. 19:18 NLT). The promise is "Train up a child in the way he should go, even when he is old he will not depart from it" (Prov. 22:6 NASB). Sound instruction and proper discipline, along with godly example, will help ensure that your children honor God throughout their lifetimes.

***

The great love chapter, 1 Corinthians 13, tells us that love is not easily provoked. It can take so little to provoke us. There are times when we pounce on a minor word or action by a spouse, child, friend, or stranger, and almost relish or enjoy being provoked. We let a little provocation grow into seething inner resentment or verbal outbursts of anger. We must not allow ourselves to be easily provoked. It hurts us and it hurts others. It is not honoring to God and it requires an apology.

Parents can be too easily provoked by their children and fly into a tirade over a minor incident. Don't reprimand your children over every little thing they do. Save up for the big things—they'll come.

Parents are not the only ones who can be provoked. Children can be provoked by their parents. God has a special admonition for dads: "Fathers, do not provoke your children to anger by the way you treat them. Rather, bring them up with the discipline and

Forgiveness: The Key to a Happy Family

instruction that comes from the Lord" (Eph. 6:4 NLT). Parents can confuse and discourage their children with unfair and inconsistent punishment. Discipline needs to be fair and consistent, and never administered in anger.

Remember that you teach your children by your example—it is not fair or consistent to require more of them than you do of yourself. Do you lie and expect them to tell the truth? Do you yell at them and then demand that they speak softly? Do you expect them to apologize when they've never heard you say, "I'm sorry"? Do you pass by the poor and then expect your children to be compassionate and generous? If your children are going to exemplify godly behavior, they need to see that you hold yourself to the same high standards.

One way parents can set an example that honors God is in our love for others. In his book *Harmony of the Gospels in Rhyming Verse*, Roland S. Taylor paraphrases Luke 10:25–28:

> An expert on the law approached one day,
> To learn if Christ and Moses would agree.
> He asked the Lord to specify the way
> To gain celestial life, eternally.
>
> Christ asked him to recount the Moses part,
> So he complied with texts he chose to tell;
> "You need to love the Lord with all your heart,
> Your soul, your strength, and with your mind as well.
>
> And you must love your neighbor, the same way
> You love yourself," Christ heard the lawyer quote;
> So Jesus did not hesitate to say,
> That he agreed with what the prophet wrote.

Jesus goes on to tell what we have come to call the story of the good Samaritan, where the priest and the Levite pass by the wounded man on the side of the Jericho road.

We want to think that we are like the Samaritan who came to the wounded man's aid, but in reality we are all too often like the

Forgiveness: The Key to Lasting Joy

priest and the Levite. We need to ask God's forgiveness for our indifference to the needs of hurting humanity.

There are countless references in the Bible for Christians to care for the poor: "Blessed is he who considers the poor; the LORD will deliver him in time of trouble" (Ps. 41:1). Jesus tells us that when we serve the poor, we serve Him. When we neglect the poor, we neglect Him.

Our son-in-law, Jack, thought of a special project to involve his two little girls in helping the poor who stand at intersections asking for food. Together they pack plastic bags with wrapped crackers, dried fruit, and nuts, along with a message telling of God's love. I call them "Jack Packs," even though he doesn't want me to, because it was Jack who came up with the idea of preparing these gifts to give to the needy.

Our daughter, Dawn, and our granddaughters, along with multitudes of other caring people, purchase gifts and pack them for needy children as part of the Samaritan's Purse Christmas Child Shoebox Ministry.

These are tangible ways to teach children obedience to God's Word to care for the poor and to experience the joy that comes to cheerful givers. Lessons that are taught verbally and also put into practice will most likely last a lifetime.

The smallest child can drop a coin in the Salvation Army's kettle at Christmas and experience the joy of giving. Children who are encouraged to do so will find for themselves the truth Jesus told us: "It is more blessed to give than to receive" (Acts 20:35b NASB).

"Christ is the head of this house, the unseen guest at every meal, the silent listener to every conversation." This was a motto that hung on the wall in Roland's boyhood home, but it was more than a motto. Christ was truly the head of the house in Colombia, South America, where James and Martha Taylor served as missionaries.

James Taylor was greatly involved in winning the Colombians to faith in Christ, but he didn't neglect his own children. Roland

Forgiveness: The Key to a Happy Family

remembers a very important day when at the age of eight he was with his father in their home's Spanish-style patio. His father gave him the greatest gift he could have bestowed on his son. He explained to Roland that he was a sinner and needed to ask God to forgive him and to give him a new life in Christ. Roland asked Jesus to come into his heart. From that day onward, Roland never doubted that he belonged to Jesus and that he would go to heaven when he died.

It was a short time later that his father became ill with an infection caused by a spider bite. He died and was buried in Barranquilla, Colombia. Roland's mother was left with five little children and one on the way. The sailors helped Roland celebrate his ninth birthday on the ship returning home to Southern California.

Christ continued to be the head of the house after Roland's father died and his family returned to the United States. His mother, without a regular income, provided physical and spiritual sustenance for her six children. She had the help of grandparents and other caring Christians. She never let her children forget that God was the source of everything needed and enjoyed.

Roland recalls a time when he showed his mom a big hole in the sole of his shoe. She got out her wallet and showed him that there was no money in it. There was, however, what looked like a check. It was written on the Bank of Heaven, with these words: "My God shall supply all your needs according to His riches in glory by Christ Jesus." She asked him to pray that God would provide the money for a new pair of shoes. He did, and the shoes arrived in good time. Roland knew they were evidence of God's love and care for him.

Mother Taylor also tried to instill self-reliance in her children. Roland's older brother was the first to contribute to the family income. He got up early every morning to deliver newspapers. Roland's first job was selling magazines at a busy intersection. When he was able to buy a bicycle, he put it to work delivering newspapers. He arose daily at three a.m. to deliver two routes.

Forgiveness: The Key to Lasting Joy

I remember standing on a stool scooping ice cream in my parents' soda fountain at a very early age, so I like to describe my childhood in the superlative title of a book I want to write: *Whipped Cream and a Cherry on Top!*

Although my family never had prayer or Bible-reading in our home, and we never attended church as a family, our parents were totally committed to each other and to their children. People used to say, "His word is his bond," and the entire community knew that this was true of my father, Bill Smith, as well as of my mother, Thelma Smith. Somehow my parents provided a strong moral compass for all six of their children.

My brothers and sisters and I were blessed by our Christian grandmother's influence. Whenever she visited, she would sit at the sewing machine, singing hymns while she made new clothes for us. The summer before I entered high school, my focus in life changed when my aunt led me to the Lord. From that time on, I knew I wanted Christ to be the center of my life and the head of my home.

When Roland and I married, we were serious about making Christ the center of our home. Although we were very busy with a growing church and my teaching at a nearby elementary school, we always realized that our most important responsibility was to be the best Christian parents we could be. We continually prayed for guidance in raising our children.

We weren't perfect parents, and our children weren't perfect either. You might have heard about the antics of P.K.'s (preacher's kids). Of course, we attributed any improper behavior to the fact that our children played with the deacons' kids. That's all in the past now, because our children are grown. And we have finally achieved success: we have perfect grandchildren. (Of course, I'm just kidding about the deacons' kids and the perfect grandchildren! But our grandchildren are *nearly* perfect, in our eyes anyway.)

Our children must think they turned out all right because they asked us to write a book on raising a family. We told them we couldn't do that because it would put too much pressure on them to be good for the rest of their lives (and that is also written with a grin).

Forgiveness: The Key to a Happy Family

As you read this chapter, you may be thinking that your spouse has already drained your forgiveness cup dry even if you've just been married for a year or two. Just wait until you have children! With each one, and at every stage in their lives, you will be tested. You and your spouse may have differences as to what form of discipline is appropriate for infractions of your household rules and your moral code, but whatever you do, don't let your children know of your disagreements. They will be very quick to play one of you against the other.

You may not see eye to eye with your spouse or your children as to the choice of their friends, their sports activities, household chores, or yard work. You may have issues with how much they need compared to what they want. As they get older, you will have to decide if giving them an allowance is the right thing to do and, if so, how much is appropriate for different ages.

Just wait until you have teenagers in the house! There will be many calls for you to forgive your children and for them to forgive you as you work through those challenging years. With lots of prayer, patience, forgiveness, and a sense of humor, you'll even survive their driving and dating years. And you'll find the joys of parenting certainly outweigh the problems.

We often treat the ones we love the most, the worst. What must our children think when we are kind and thoughtful to friends and even strangers, but in our own home we are abusive and unkind? There should be a kindness key that unlocks the door to our home.

Harmony in the home is maintained through kindness and forgiveness. We need to learn and live the verse, "Be kind to one another, tenderhearted, forgiving one another, just as God in Christ also forgave you" (Eph. 4:32).

The best way for parents to teach kindness and forgiveness is by modeling it for their children. There's a saying, "Your actions speak so loud I can't hear a word you say." When you fail, don't be afraid to ask your children to forgive you. They also need to

Forgiveness: The Key to Lasting Joy

hear their parents ask forgiveness from each other if they've heard them in an argument.

Children learn to say "please" and "thank you" and "I love you" at a very early age. They also need to be taught to say "I'm sorry" when they do something unkind.

Sibling rivalry is present in every home except those where there's only one child. The Bible relates a number of cases where such rivalry was carried to the extreme. The first example is that of Cain, who murdered his brother Abel because of jealousy.

Another story of sibling rivalry in the book of Genesis has a happier ending. Jacob and Esau, sons of Isaac and Rebekah, had very different talents and personalities. Their parents weren't very wise in the way they related to their boys. Isaac favored Esau, while Jacob was a mama's boy. When it came time for Isaac to give the blessing of birthright to Esau, Rebekah devised a scheme so that Jacob would get the blessing. Isaac was tricked into giving the blessing to his second son instead of his firstborn, as was the custom.

Esau's anger was so great when he learned that his brother had cheated him out of his inheritance that he plotted to kill Jacob. When Rebekah became aware of Esau's plan, she helped her favorite flee for his life.

After twenty years of living in fear of Esau, Jacob got up the courage to send word to his brother that he was coming to see him. As Jacob approached, Esau ran to meet him. They wept as they embraced and kissed each other. What a beautiful story of love and forgiveness!

Joseph—famous for his coat of many colors—was pampered by his father. His ten older brothers resented the favor he was shown and looked on him as a spoiled brat. They sold him as a slave to a caravan that took him to Egypt. In God's providence, Joseph was elevated to a position of authority second only to Pharaoh.

Forgiveness: The Key to a Happy Family

Meanwhile there was a great famine in the land of Egypt and the surrounding countries, including Canaan, where Jacob and his family lived. They were on the verge of starvation when they learned that there was grain available in Egypt, so Jacob sent his sons to buy provisions.

Pharaoh had placed Joseph in charge of all the granaries. When the ten brothers came, Joseph recognized them immediately, but he hid his identity from them. It was not until the youngest, Benjamin, was brought before Joseph that he revealed himself to them. He said, "I am Joseph, your brother whom you sold into Egypt! But don't be angry with yourselves that you did this to me, for God did it! He sent me here ahead of you to preserve your lives" (Gen. 45:4–5 TLB).

Joseph kissed and embraced each of his brothers and forgave them all. He then arranged with Pharaoh to bring his father and all his clan to live in the fertile region of Goshen. When Jacob arrived with all his possessions, the family unity was made complete.

There is no more compelling story of genuine forgiveness in Hebrew literature than Joseph's story. In fact, theologians often refer to Joseph as the most Christlike person in the Old Testament.

The cause of sibling rivalry can often be traced to unwise parenting. Favoritism, whether real or imagined, can cause jealousy and excessive competition. Some competition among siblings is good, but no child should feel unloved because his brother or sister is better looking, is more intellectually advanced, or possesses unique talents. Each child should feel secure in your love. In my family I think each of the six of us felt we were the favorite. Our parents made all of us feel we were special.

Our two sons, who are exactly one year apart, were very close friends growing up, but they were also very competitive. They tried to outdo each other in chess, in Monopoly, in who read the greatest number of books, in wrestling, in golf, and in music. Steve played the trombone and Jim played the trumpet in their school band. Perhaps a greater competitive spirit in music could have caused them to practice more!

Forgiveness: The Key to Lasting Joy

Once, when a verbal exchange between them became more heated than usual, I interjected myself into their argument. I like to think I always had the good sense to stay out of their quarrels, unless it was to tell them both to cease and refrain. In this incident, however, I thought Steve had gone too far in insulting his brother so I popped in with, "Well, you're not such a good catch either."

I had no thought that Steve would take my words seriously and think that I actually meant them, but years later he reminded me of what I had said. While trying to encourage Jim, I had deeply hurt and discouraged Steve. I was devastated that I had hurt him, and I sincerely apologized. It brings me almost to tears to write about those careless words I thoughtlessly spoke. We all need to pray David's prayer: "Set a guard, O LORD, over my mouth; keep watch over the door of my lips" (Ps. 141:3).

By the way, our sons are both great catches who have long since been caught. They are great friends, too.

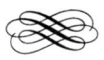

There are times when some of us are too thin skinned. We ourselves need to remember, and we need to teach our children that we should not let other people's thoughtless words or actions discourage us. It is possible for us to take ourselves too seriously and to wear our feelings on our sleeves, as the saying goes. There are comments or incidents that hurt us or even give us cause to be offended, but we still must guard our reactions.

A farmer hurt the feelings of a fourteen-year-old boy who lived on the adjoining farm. The boy was so upset that he could not sleep that night. He tried to think of some way he could get even. It was nearly dawn when an idea came to him.

Early that morning he mounted his horse and rode twenty miles to purchase a bag of Johnson grass seed. After dark he sowed his neighbor's richest bottomland with the seed. Now, if you're a farmer, you know you can fight Johnson grass most of your lifetime without killing it. So the grass came up, and the neighbor fought Johnson grass until he died.

Forgiveness: The Key to a Happy Family

In the meantime, the boy grew up and fell in love with the neighbor's daughter. They were married, and when the farmer died he left the farm to his daughter. The man who sowed the field in his youth said, "For over forty years I've fought Johnson grass."

The words of Eliphaz, found in the oldest book of the Bible, are true: "Those who plow iniquity and sow trouble, reap the same" (Job 4:8).

Sometimes we have to bite our tongues to keep from responding to a perceived insult with an angry retort that will fuel an explosive situation. We may grit our teeth and count to ten, but we must do so behind closed lips. Let's remind ourselves that if we can't say something helpful, we shouldn't say anything at all. "Help me, Lord, to keep my mouth shut and my lips sealed" (Psalm 141:3 TLB).

I should realize I have a choice to make. Will I let that thoughtless comment or action offend me? No, I choose not to be offended.

My dad thought that learning to take teasing was a big part of our education. He had a great sense of humor and he loved a good practical joke. My brothers and sisters and I learned at an early age to take teasing and to give it. There were times when we got carried away and someone got his or her feelings hurt. It was then that our tenderhearted mother had to provide comfort and call for a truce and an apology.

Temper tantrums and outbursts of anger are not only disruptive and damaging to your home's peace and tranquility, but they are very harmful to children and adults who do not learn to control their temper.

I had a student in my third grade class who was very smart and likeable, but he had a terrible problem with his uncontrollable temper. On more than one occasion he attacked one of his classmates and appeared to be trying to choke him. I had to physically pull him off because there was no time to call the principal.

This boy, whose name I remember very well, was in anger management counseling for a number of years. His mother was very supportive of my effort to help her son. I've often thought of the great potential this young man had. Although I lost touch, I've always wanted to believe that he conquered his anger and went on to achieve great things in life.

It's been said that Dwight D. Eisenhower—five-star general, commander of the Allied Forces in Europe, and thirty-fourth president of the United States—had a serious problem with anger during his childhood. When he was a boy living in Kansas, where the Eisenhower Library is today, he often got into fights.

One day, when his godly mother was caring for his injuries, she recited: "He who is slow to anger is better than the mighty, and he who rules his spirit than he who takes a city" (Prov. 16:32). When this great leader of men and country was reflecting over his life, he wrote about the time his mother impressed that verse on his mind: "I have always looked back on that conversation as one of the most valuable moments of my life."

In the old days, churches didn't pay preachers too well. The saying used to be, "Lord, You keep him humble, we'll keep him poor." Some tenderhearted parishioners tried to compensate for the lack of a livable salary in unique ways. One generous form of compensation was a "pounding." We weren't sure we wanted to be pounded, but when gifts of flour, sugar, honey, coffee, and candy were brought in by the pound, we decided that an old-fashioned pounding was great.

Our two-bedroom, one-bath parsonage had very little storage space, so we built shelves in the children's closet to store our abundant supplies. All went well until our precious little toddlers discovered the loot. Steve, our oldest, found a five-pound bag of sugar, and after eating all he wanted and sharing it with his brother, he sprinkled it all over the bedroom. We attribute the discovery of a five-pound bag of flour to Jim, who made the room look like a white Christmas. We like to blame Dawn for getting into a big jar of honey. Whether she was the chief culprit or not, the evidence

Forgiveness: The Key to a Happy Family

pointed to her tiny little feet dancing around the room, tracking the sticky stuff everywhere.

Even after those messes, it's amazing how time and perspective have transformed those dramatic events into some of the sweetest memories of our children's preschool years.

It was from that same bedroom that little Jimmy emerged one day when I was entertaining a group of ladies. With a big smile on his face, he announced, "Mommy, I gave Dawn a butch." He certainly had. With a little pair of plastic scissors he had cut her hair to the scalp. His sister seemed equally happy with her brother's achievement. Dawn proudly showed the ladies her new haircut. Dawn's hair was very blonde and slow in coming in when she was a baby, so Beverly, a dear lady in the church, made little frilly dresses with matching bonnets so people wouldn't mistake our little daughter as a third son.

What many have dubbed "The Terrible Twos" I call "The Terrific Twos." Of course, now that I'm a grandmother and no longer the mother of a two-year-old, it's easy to see the little darlings in their best light.

We recall a time when young Jimmy disobeyed us. His father reprimanded him and sent him to his room. After what seemed to us just a few minutes, Dawn came to her father and asked, "Daddy, don't you think it's time to tell Jimmy it's OK?" She knew it was our practice to bring any punishment to a conclusion. In her mind, it was time for Dad to hug Jimmy and let him know he was forgiven.

Although Dawn was younger than her brothers, she kept a watchful eye over them throughout the years. When those she perceived to be the wrong kind of girls showed an interest in her brothers, she was like a little mother, always ready to protect them from dating the ones she thought weren't good enough for them.

We enjoy reminiscing about our children and grandchildren, who, like all children, seem to grow up too fast.

Our first family European holiday was preceded by lengthy preparation. It was a challenge to pack lightly for twenty-one days with a family of five. We also gave a lot of thought to obtaining the best camera for the occasion.

Forgiveness: The Key to Lasting Joy

We landed in Frankfurt and picked up our rental car, a compact vehicle. We loaded our luggage in the trunk and placed the two adults in the front and three preteens into the cramped back-seat. We set off, eager to show our children as much of Europe as possible in our three-week time frame. We knew it would be the experience of a lifetime and we were eager to keep a photographic record of every site we visited.

Our first destination was Heidelberg University and castle, picturesquely situated on the beautiful Rhine River. We took some perfect shots of our children appropriately posing in front of the castle and the bridge over the Rhine. We climbed up the long, steep, grassy slope that led to the treasures within the castle. After we had taken numerous shots of historic significance, our older son, Steve, asked if he could carry the camera and take some of the pictures.

The children couldn't resist running down the hill. Roland called out, "Be careful, Steve, or you'll fall and break the camera."

Oblivious to the warning, Steve continued down the hillside, gaining speed with every step of his lanky body. What seemed like the inevitable happened. We were concerned about his skinned knees and even more concerned about the camera. Steve showed us the camera and we were convinced it wasn't broken. He knew he deserved a strong reprimand, but not a word was said about the camera, only gratitude that he wasn't injured because of the fall.

The day finally arrived after the trip when our slides were developed. With eager anticipation, the family waited for Dad to set up the screen and load the carousel. The light from the projector revealed some beautiful scenes of Heidelberg and our three children posed in front of the castle, and on the famous bridge over the Rhine River. Those pictures were everything we hoped for, but the next slide was a disappointment, it was totally out of focus. The one that followed was equally distorted, as was the next and the next. Roland and I began to laugh. Our children could not see anything humorous about the dark blur that appeared every time a slide was

Forgiveness: The Key to a Happy Family

advanced. We explained that the camera was broken when Steve slipped and fell. We reminded them of an old expression, "Don't cry over spilt milk." Since we didn't want to cry over the ruined camera, the best thing we could do was to laugh.

For some reason that event made an indelible impression on Steve. Years later when he became the youth pastor of the church where his father was senior minister, he often referred to that incident. He knew he had been forgiven, and he had received that forgiveness with gratitude.

When we recently told Steve that we were writing a book on forgiveness, he asked that we include the preceding incident in our manuscript.

To recognize the twenty-fifth anniversary of Roland's ministry at Crossroads Baptist Church, the congregation arranged a surprise celebration. We were inundated with gifts and letters of recognition—even one from the president of the United States at the time, Ronald Reagan. As part of the celebration, the good folks of the church seated their pastor on the platform and announced, "This is your life, Pastor Roland Taylor."

Numerous friends who had enriched his life appeared as if by magic to bring greetings from far away and long ago. Roland was overwhelmed with gratitude for each of these.

By this time, Steve was impacting the lives of thousands of young people with his unique musical recordings and performances. His concerts took him to many parts of the Unites States, Europe, and South America. Despite his busy schedule, Steve secretly appeared at the piano, accompanying himself in a song he composed for the occasion, titled "Father's Song." He was the highlight of the celebration, and his song continues to be a source of blessing to us today.

Forgiveness: The Key to Lasting Joy

Father's Song
by Steve Taylor

Memories are hard to hold,
the time slips by so fast.
But lessons learned, they never leave,
although the memory's passed.
There'd always be a moral in
your stories that I'd hear.
And from watching you I could understand
'cause you'd make the message clear.

And if a picture's worth a thousand words then
your life could write a book.
Though you've moved your mountains it's the
little things that I cannot overlook.
And as a young boy sitting on his daddy's knee,
still my words come from the heart.

In my father's eyes I think I see a little bit of God.

Memories are hard to hold,
The time slips by so fast.
But lessons learned, they never leave,
although the memory's passed
And I guess I'll never realize
all the difference made by you,
till with a family I'll be looking back,
and I'll think what Dad would do.

Roland remembers an incident in Colombia, South America, when his family was having breakfast on their patio. His mother poured his dad's coffee and it was full of grounds. His father quipped, "This is grounds for complaint."

Forgiveness: The Key to a Happy Family

Years later, based on that memory, Roland developed a Thanksgiving song and slide program called "Grounds for Gratitude." He showed it in churches and service clubs for years.

Gratitude is a major contributor to a happy home. It can triumph over greed and grumbling. Parents teach their children gratitude by attitude—theirs. We will be blessed if we thank God every day for our forgiveness through Christ. The psalmist admonishes us "to declare Your lovingkindness in the morning, and Your faithfulness every night" (Ps. 92:2).

When our family gets together, we like to enumerate our blessings. We join in thanking the Lord for giving us so much. Then our prayer is, "Give us one thing more: grateful hearts."

My husband has a song in his heart ready to break forth audibly for every occasion or situation. I can't imagine our home without music to express our praise to God, our joys, our sorrows, our love, and even our repentance. Singing has been an important part of our daily life and devotions.

When our children, and later our grandchildren, were little, we sang choruses and hymns with them at home and in the car. Our grandchildren thought the first thing they should do when they got buckled into their car seats was to sing at the top of their voices, "This is the day that the Lord has made, we will rejoice and be glad in it."

We should all have a song of thanksgiving in our hearts and on our lips. Appreciation to God and to our family promotes genuine happiness throughout the day. A song, a cheerful smile, a word of thanks, and a soft answer are welcome in the home at any time, but when we fail in our loving relationships, we need to ask for forgiveness and begin again. This is a new day that the Lord has made. We will rejoice and be glad in it. Expressions of appreciation and gratitude are necessary building blocks for constructing a happy home.

There have been days when we have failed to have a positive attitude and a song in our hearts. You've probably had those days too. It is at such times that our song needs to be one of repentance.

Forgiveness: The Key to Lasting Joy

Maude Battersby wrote the following lyrics, and we have sung them often as our prayer:

If I have wounded any soul today,
If I have caused one foot to go astray,
If I have gone in my own willful way,
Dear Lord, forgive.

Forgive the sins I have confessed to Thee,
Forgive the secret sins I do not see.
O guide me, love me and my keeper be
Dear Lord, forgive.

Edmond Burke was one of the most interesting figures in American history. I believe it was he who visited Washington, D.C., and wrote an editorial in which he said, "The stars in their courses could not look down upon a more magnificent site than the capitol of our republic. This is the secret of America's greatness; this is the secret of her success."

A short time later, however, he was invited to the home of a friend who lived on a farm. He joined the family seated around a sumptuously laden table. His host offered a prayer of thanks for the food as the family bowed their heads in gratitude.

When they had finished eating they went to the living room, where the father read a portion from the Bible. Each member of the family gave thanks for God's protection during the day and asked Him for a good night's rest.

Then the children scampered off to bed, while the father went out to take care of some chores. Mother went to the kitchen to wash the dishes, and Mr. Burke went to his room to write another editorial. He said, "I was wrong. The secret of America's greatness is not found in her legislative halls of government, but in homes where God is honored and where children are taught reliance on the Almighty."

Forgiveness: The Key to a Happy Family

Our son-in-law likes mother-in-law jokes. I'm not crazy about them. In fact, I didn't even like the TV show *Everybody Loves Raymond* because they portrayed the mother-in-law as such an obnoxious character.

We were on a cruise with our children and grandchildren and I was on my way up to the buffet where we all met much too often. The elevator door opened, and there was Jack in the back of the crowd. He said, "I don't think we have room for this old lady." People looked at him with such hostility that I thought they were about to attack him. I laughed and said, "Oh, he's my son-in-law."

I've thought since, I should have kept quiet and let them knock his block off. Then maybe he would learn to treat me with the respect I deserve! (The truth is, he's a great guy and we love him like our own sons.)

It's important that in-laws not be too possessive or interfere in their married children's lives. It's easy to want to help too much or give unsolicited advice. We need to be careful.

In Matthew and Mark, Jesus quotes Genesis 2:24: "Therefore a man shall leave his father and mother and be joined to his wife, and they will become one flesh." In Matthew 19:5–6 and again in Mark 10:7–8, Jesus adds, "So they are no longer two, but one. Therefore, what God has joined together, let man not separate" (NIV).

The in-laws must never become a wedge between their son or daughter and that child's spouse. Your children are much more likely to include you in their family activities if you don't push yourself on them. It is important to remember that they need time with just the two of them and their children. When we overstep as in-laws, a sincere apology is most appropriate.

Maybe it's because I'm a minister's wife, but people often tell me their personal stories of divisions in their families. It surprises me that there are so many conflicts between family members.

Many of the rifts in families begin with disagreements over a trinket or a harsh word. There may have been perceived favoritism between siblings or arguments over inheritance. Even a minor incident can lead to a lifetime break in relationships where siblings or parents don't talk to each other.

You may think you are justified in your anger because your dispute was over something of great value or importance, but whatever it was, it isn't worth the cost of a broken family relationship.

Roland and I know of too many painful family rifts. One of them came to a head at a wedding. The bride-to-be, who for years had felt abandoned by her father, asked him to walk her down the aisle at her wedding. The father, who had felt rejected by his daughter, agreed to the arrangement and even consented to buy her wedding gown. Then came the conflict over the price of the dress. He felt it was too expensive and refused to pay for it. Many harsh words and hurt feelings followed.

The bride was married in her beautiful white gown, but her father didn't attend her wedding. The rift between father and daughter widened, and at this writing, they still have not reconciled. He has no association with his daughter and his grandchildren. Both of them feel justified in their anger and resentment toward each other.

Harboring resentment is not healthy for the body or the soul. The question is, who will be the one to reach out with a simple but sincere apology? A broken relationship results in too many wasted years of separation. It's time to heal the hurting heart.

There is nothing to be gained by failure to forgive. It isn't productive to be historical and bring out all of the past years' injustices. There may never be resolution of your differences, but there can be reconciliation and restoration of the relationship.

It's important that we not be rigid in thinking that an apology must be a verbal "I'm sorry." Perhaps you could begin with a card, but do make some gesture to open communication again. Accept any positive response in return. If you don't get a response the first time, try again.

There are times when we apologize and we don't get the apology we had hoped for or thought we deserved, but welcome and accept what is offered anyway. Remember, you aren't looking for

Forgiveness: The Key to a Happy Family

retribution or restitution, but a restored relationship. Wouldn't it be wonderful if you let God use you as the peacemaker in your family?

I watched my granddaughter swim at the clubhouse pool and jotted down thoughts for our forgiveness book. Ideas seemed to come quickly.

"Are you writing your memoirs?" I heard.

I looked up at a dripping wet stranger. "No, I'm writing a book about forgiveness."

Without hesitation the inquisitive man told me that he was trying to forgive his dead mother. He said he'd made progress, but sometimes the cruel things she did to him and to his six brothers and sisters came back to him. The conversation led me to ask if there'd been any forgiveness while she was alive. He said there hadn't been.

He said, "My sister told me I should consider the hard things in my mother's life that had made her the way she was. I asked her if she could ever treat her children so harshly, just because she had been mistreated."

I told him that the recognition of God's great forgiveness through Christ for my own personal sin helps me to forgive others. He acknowledged that truth and said he was trying to forgive. As he was leaving, he said, "There are books about every subject, but I've never heard of one about forgiveness. I'd like to read your book."

Unfortunately there are many people who carry emotional scars from being mistreated or abused as children. They can't change the past and they may not be able to forget, but with God's help they can forgive. They can learn from the past and determine that their children will have a happy home.

People really want to have the burden of unforgiveness lifted from their life. It does take courage to ask for forgiveness because there is a fear that our apology will be rejected. True, we aren't assured that our apology will be accepted, but when we do our part there is a peace that comes to us and we can leave the results in God's hands.

What is the right response when you think an apology is insincere? We recently heard of a teenage boy who was caught stealing money from his relatives. This caused the rift between him and his already broken family to grow wider.

He finally wrote a note of apology to two family members, but because of his history of lying, cheating, and stealing, they doubted his sincerity and made no response to his apology.

Of course, it isn't easy to forgive when there's a pattern of deception, but it is not our place to judge the motives or sincerity behind an apology. This boy could have written his apology with a sincere desire to be reinstated into the family circle, or he may have been insincere and only trying to manipulate the family. Only God can know his heart.

It is not the Christian's responsibility to judge whether an apology is sincere. We are required before God to forgive in the way God has forgiven us. We often pray the Lord's Prayer with our request that God will "forgive us our debts as we forgive our debtors." Our response to an apology should be, "Apology accepted, forgiveness granted."

Paul appealed in his second letter to the Corinthians for them to forgive a man in their church who had been punished for immoral behavior. He wrote, "Most of you opposed him, and that was punishment enough. Now, however, it is time to forgive and comfort him. Otherwise he may be overcome by discouragement. So I urge you now to reaffirm your love for him" (2 Cor. 2:6–8 NLT). This applies to churches and to families. Now is the time to forgive.

A shadow of sadness fell over our group of usually cheerful volunteers when we learned that the son of one of our friends had suddenly died. When we took a coffee break, the lady sitting across from me told me that she too had lost a son. With tears

Forgiveness: The Key to a Happy Family

in her eyes, she said, "He was my firstborn child." I shed some tears with her.

This lovely lady unburdened her heart to me. "I wasn't a good mom. I yelled at my children, I was constantly complaining about their behavior and even their character. I was far more interested in keeping my house clean than I was in playing with my children." She went on to tell me that her marriage hadn't been good because her husband drank excessively.

I listened with empathy and patted her hand. She went on to say, "But I'm a good grandma. I never have a cross word for my grandchildren. I let them scatter toys all over the house and I love to play with them and do things for them. They're the center of my life."

As I tried to encourage my friend, I said, "It's not too late to tell your children just what you've told me. Tell them you're sorry that you were preoccupied with unimportant things when they were growing up and you failed to play with them and enjoy their childhood years. Apologize to them. They'll understand and it will be a great lesson for them in raising their own children."

My friend regretted the kind of mom she'd been, but she's proud of the kind of grandmother she is. God used even her regrets and sorrow to shape her life and make her the beautiful person she is today.

In regard to our extended family, we need to show our children that as adults we continue to honor our parents. It's also important that there be harmony in the larger family circle of our brothers' and sisters' families. My husband's family and mine look forward to the times we can be together. Grandparents, aunts, uncles, and cousins should have very congenial relationships.

If you, as a parent, want your children to continue to spend time with you and their brothers and sisters when they are adults, they need to see that it is important to their mom and dad to stay close to their families.

Forgiveness: The Key to Lasting Joy

My sisters and I were all with my mother when she was in failing health. She asked us to continue to get together after she was gone. We have been blessed to do so and have included our brothers and their families in great family celebrations. Families shouldn't wait for weddings and funerals to enjoy each other's company.

It's very important to my husband and me to get our children all together at least once a year. In the horse-and-buggy days it wasn't possible for families like ours spread across the country to do this, but with today's transportation and communication, family reunions should be a priority.

We're not a perfect family, but we're a forgiven family. Each one of us has received God's forgiveness through Christ and we want to be a forgiving family. God forgave us and He wants us to forgive each other.

We know that possessions and accomplishments don't mean much when there is animosity in the family. We don't measure our success as parents by the wealth, fame, or education our children gain, but by children and grandchildren who love each other and love the Lord.

The best advice we can give as survivors of raising toddlers, teens, and in-betweens is to pray and forgive. When your child turns thirteen, you're moving into uncharted territory. He or she has never been a teenager before. Parents, pray for your teenage children. Teens, pray for your parents and forgive each other. Remember, we're all a work in progress and God isn't finished with us yet.

Raising a family is wonderful in retrospect. We've found that we remember lots of happy, funny little experiences we've had with our children as they were growing up, but we've forgotten the negative experiences.

The empty nest syndrome that many couples fear is really a blessing once the initial shock of so much peace and quiet is gone. More time for each other, more money, less laundry, and more food in the fridge can't be all bad. Of course, their phone calls and visits are always welcome interruptions.

I thought my whipped-cream-with-a-cherry-on-top life just couldn't get any better. God's forgiveness, a great husband,

Forgiveness: The Key to a Happy Family

wonderful children who all have terrific mates—what more could there be? Grandchildren!

How blessed we are. What a life we've had. It's all been because we found the key to a happy family: forgiveness.

Your Turn

1. How can I achieve the proper balance in teaching my children the fear of God and God's love and forgiveness?

2. What are some ways I can restore a close relationship with my children after I have punished them?

3. How can I model kindness and forgiveness to my children?

3

Forgiveness: The Key to Harmony in the Church

WHAT IS THE church? The church is people—not perfect people, but forgiven people. We're not people who think we're good or better than those outside the church, but people who know we're not good and are asking for God's mercy. We've come to God, God's way. It's the way of the cross. God sent His perfect Son to die on the cross to pay the penalty for our sins. We admit our sins to Him, ask His forgiveness, and gratefully receive it. Forgiveness is the key to the church and the key to heaven.

A little boy was lost in the heart of London. He was near the area of Charing Cross, which is referred to locally as "the Cross." A London police officer came upon the lost child, who was unable to tell him his address. Finally, through his sobs and tears, the little boy said, "If you take me to the Cross, I'm sure I can find my way home." The police officer took the child to the Cross and he was soon united with his grateful parents. On hearing this story, Jessie Brown Pound wrote the famous hymn:

> I must needs go home by the way of the cross,
> There's no other way but this.
> I shall ne'er get sight of the Gates of Light,
> If the way of the cross I miss.

Forgiveness: The Key to Lasting Joy

> The way of the cross leads home,
> The way of the cross leads home.
> It is sweet to know, as I onward go,
> The way of the cross leads home.

The church has withstood persecution from without and failures from within because it is built on the firm foundation of Jesus Christ and His death on the cross. It was at Caesarea Philippi that Jesus declared to His apostles, "I will build my church; and the gates of hell shall not prevail against it" (Matt. 16:18b KJV).

The church continues to be relevant and necessary for proclaiming the message of forgiveness to the world. It is and has been all about forgiveness. It is comprised of individuals who are forgiven and want to share the message of God's forgiveness with others. The church is a little group of believers meeting underground, or it is the mega church or great cathedral. Any place where believers are gathered together to worship the living Lord can be the church. It can have a preacher with a seminary degree or a lay leader faithfully teaching God's Word.

We are blessed in the United States to be able to freely attend any church we choose. We should never forget to pray for persecuted believers who risk their lives to join with other Christians in underground house churches. Instruction in God's Word is so important to them that they are willing to face beatings and imprisonment to join with other Christians in fellowship and worship.

Some people take a very casual view of church attendance. Some proclaim that the great outdoors is their church or that they can worship God on the golf course. But they miss the significance of what the church is. It isn't all about you; it isn't all about me. It is about our worship, our service, and our obedience to God. His Word tells us, "Let us not neglect our church meetings as some people do" (Heb. 10:25a TLB).

We shouldn't choose a church just because it makes us feel good or entertains us, like going to a concert or a theater. We've heard people say, "I didn't get anything out of the service." That misses the point. We go to church to worship and we depart to serve. The

Forgiveness: The Key to Harmony in the Church

church's mission is found in the Great Commission: "Go therefore and make disciples of all nations, baptizing them in the name of the Father and the Son and the Holy Spirit" (Matt. 28:19 NASB).

The local church we attend should challenge and equip us to obey the Great Commission to spread the good news of God's forgiveness through Christ in our community and throughout the earth. John 3:16 reminds us that "God so loved the world, that He gave his only begotten Son, that whoever believes in Him should not perish, but have eternal life" (NASB).

The church should never lose sight of its responsibility to introduce people to the Lord. In doing this, we are called to show God's love by providing for the physical needs of a hurting humanity. The church is a place of caring and of sharing. There are many areas where churches can work together to provide for the hungry and destitute in the community. The Bible says, "God blesses those who are kind to the poor. He helps them out of their troubles. He protects them and keeps them alive. He publicly honors them when they are sick, and soothes their pain and worries" (Psalm 41:1–2a TLB).

Too often the churches in a community fail to cooperate because of denominational differences. One little girl asked her friend, "Why don't you attend the same church we go to?"

Her friend responded, "I think it's because we belong to a different abomination."

There are those who carry their denominational differences to an extreme. It's like the person who says, "I am a member of the only true church, of which I am the sole surviving member."

During his twenty-nine years as pastor of Crossroads Church, Roland had the privilege of visiting dozens of churches of various denominations in the Denver area. He arranged several programs in song and slides to celebrate Christmas, Thanksgiving, and Easter. He told people, all in one breath, "I belong to the Unitedevangelicomethobaptipalianprespigationalist church." It's a blessing to visit congregations of different theological perspectives and celebrate our faith in Jesus Christ.

Forgiveness: The Key to Lasting Joy

Many communities have been blessed when the churches join together in an evangelistic crusade. Noted evangelists such as Dwight L. Moody or Billy Sunday have had an impact on the nation in that way. Our church was blessed when the Denver metropolitan churches invited Billy Graham to preach in Mile High Stadium. Denominational differences were set aside as we gathered together to pray for the salvation of lost souls. We'll never forget the night Roland stood before the packed stadium to pray for God's blessing on the preacher and the people. Billy Graham always encouraged those who responded to the invitation to find a Bible-believing church. We rejoiced as we welcomed new believers into our churches as a result.

Evangelistic crusades are all about forgiveness. Thousands came forward in Mile High Stadium asking God to forgive their sins and accept them into His family of forgiven sinners.

A Baptist minister tells about the time Gypsy Smith, Jr. was invited to hold a tent revival in his small town. All the churches cooperated and there was a genuine revival. Two dedicated ladies even went to the edge of town to invite old Miss Sadie, a disreputable woman who was known throughout the city. If people wanted to describe a person who was living a sinful life, they would say, "He or she is as wicked as old Miss Sadie."

When these two ladies asked Miss Sadie to attend the revival service, she just laughed and said, "No one would allow me to enter the tent." Day after day the ladies returned, trying to persuade Miss Sadie to change her mind. Because of their persistence, she finally agreed to go, but she insisted that she would just sit outside the tent and listen. The two ladies sat with her several evenings, but one evening she relented, and sat in the back of the tent. When the invitation was given to come forward and receive Christ, everyone heard her shout, "Praise the Lord." The people watched with astonishment as old Miss Sadie started down the aisle. Members of the different churches—Methodist, Presbyterian, Lutheran, and Baptist—hoped she wouldn't join their church.

On Sunday morning, the Baptist church was nearing the conclusion of the worship service when old Miss Sadie entered and

Forgiveness: The Key to Harmony in the Church

started toward the front. A wave of resentment that could almost be felt swept through the congregation. *Why did she come here? What are we going to do with a person as degraded as she?*

Then something happened that was one of the most touching scenes to be played out in a church. A beautiful young lady, everybody's sweetheart and the direct antithesis of Miss Sadie, stepped out from the choir and walked down the aisle to meet her. She cupped her face in her hands and kissed her forehead. Then with her arm around her shoulder, she walked her to the front of the congregation so that she could be welcomed into the church. The spirit of resentment and revulsion was miraculously changed into one of joy and exultation as the congregation, ashamed of their initial reaction, welcomed Miss Sadie into their fellowship. From that day until the day she died, she never missed a service and her funeral was the largest the town had ever witnessed.

This is a story of forgiveness. The church people needed and received forgiveness for their pride, and Miss Sadie received forgiveness for her sinful life. They came together at the foot of the cross.

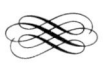

A physicist was showing his class an experiment. He had a bottle, a nail, and a board. He took the nail and drove it into the board, using the bottle as a hammer. Then holding the bottle up, he said, "This is the hardest glass that's made. You saw me hit the nail a hard blow with it; but there is no chip, no breakage. Now watch this."

He reached over and picked up a little piece of carborundum, the heaviest known metal, and dropped it into the bottle. He stepped back, shielded his face with his left hand, and once again used the bottle to strike the nail a light blow. The bottle flew into a hundred pieces.

He said, "If I were a preacher, I'd take these things into the pulpit. I'd take a piece of carborundum, a bottle, a nail, and a board, and when everyone was sufficiently curious, I'd say to them, 'You can buck all of the rough winds of life and travel the hard roads of

Forgiveness: The Key to Lasting Joy

life until you get something inside you that doesn't belong there. It might be any of a multitude of things, but nothing damages inner tranquility more than an unforgiving spirit. Then I would illustrate with the experiment you just witnessed.'"

It is true that the church isn't perfect, but it's the best organization this side of heaven. The church isn't perfect because it is made up of imperfect people. We've served as pastor and wife in four different congregations, and we've seen the change that Christ makes in hearts and lives. We can't blame Christ when we, the people, don't act like Christians. God is not to be blamed for the church's shortcomings. We need to be more like the one whose name we claim.

When we, the church, fail to live up to our high calling, we need to recognize our shortcomings, confess them to God, and correct them. Although we love the church, we can't overlook her faults. Since this book's primary focus is forgiveness, we must recognize that in individual churches and in the larger Christian community there have been and continue to be areas where we have failed. We need to confess these failures, seek forgiveness, and press forward in obedience to God's Word.

The segregated church is a disgrace, and many Christians have worked to correct it over the years. We loved welcoming those of different races into our churches. We had close fellowship with many congregations of different ethnicities, but our suburban churches were not as ethnically diverse as we would have liked. Our church in Colorado wasn't directly involved in the civil rights movement, but perhaps we should have been. If all churches, including those in the South, had spoken out sooner, the shame of segregation wouldn't have lasted so long.

God forgives the past and challenges us to unity in the present. Let's remember the words of John Oxenham's great hymn: "In Christ there is no east or west, In Him no south or north; but one great fellowship of love throughout the whole wide earth."

The early church was composed of little groups of believers. The people of that day were saying, "Behold how these brethren love one another." Because they wanted to love and be loved, they

Forgiveness: The Key to Harmony in the Church

joined themselves to these little bands of worshipers that were known as colonies of heaven. Wouldn't it be great if our churches were known today as fellowships of love?

Some individual churches and the collective church have been very timid in teaching the biblical position on homosexuality. Of course, churches must not speak out in hateful judgment. Christians are to love everyone, and Christian organizations have been at the forefront of reaching out in compassion to help heal and prevent the spread of HIV/AIDS in Africa and around the world.

There have been protests against churches that have taken a bold stand on the teaching that marriage is between a man and a woman. The tide seems to be turning and momentum is gathering to legalize same-sex marriage. The church needs to ask God's forgiveness for our fear of being called homophobic and speak with clarity on this monumental issue.

We believe that the greatest sin and shame in our country today is the killing of unborn babies. The failure of multitudes of individual Christians and the collective Christian community to do everything in our power to stop this genocide is a travesty.

The very term "pro-choice" to describe a woman's right to take the life of her baby negates the right of another human being to life. Many young women who have been persuaded to have an abortion carry the sadness of that misguided decision throughout their lives.

If we want God to bless and protect our country, we must stop the promotion of abortion. Proverbs 6:16–19 gives a list of seven things that are an abomination to the Lord. Number three is listed as "hands that shed innocent blood." There is no blood that is more innocent than that of an unborn baby.

The evangelical community was outraged when a different Reverend Taylor, pastor of a large church in downtown Denver, received widespread coverage on radio, television, and the newspapers as he voiced his support for abortion and the so-called right to choose. My pastor husband, Rev. Roland Taylor, was known as an outspoken advocate of the pro-life conviction. Since he was known for his pro-life stand, the evangelical ministers asked him to be their spokesman to promote the Christian viewpoint.

Forgiveness: The Key to Lasting Joy

A day was set for all the like-minded ministers to bring their congregations to our church. All media sources were invited to attend, and it was advertised as "The Other Taylor Speaks Out."

As was expected, there was very little media attention given to the event other than to pit these two ministers against each other, but the Christian community came together to fill the church. The ministers association declared it a resounding success. Our church continued to support pro-life rallies, and many of our members participated in peaceful protests at abortion clinics.

Although my husband thought his colleague, the other minister, was wrong about his position on abortion, he nevertheless went to see him when he was in the hospital. Roland let him know that he loved him and was praying for his recovery.

The church is called to stand firm on important moral and doctrinal issues, but there must be flexibility on insignificant or unimportant matters. In recent decades some churches' unity has been disrupted by disagreement over church music. In an effort to reach young people, many churches, ours included, introduced more lively music with the inclusion of drums and electric guitars. While retaining the traditional hymns, gospel choruses were introduced. Most people were understanding of reaching out to young people and were willing to subordinate their own preferences. However, there were those who left their long-time church to find the traditional music more to their liking.

Some of the problems between the different age groups over church music are not really generational, not the old against the young, but the agreeable against the disagreeable. We need intergenerational harmony and compromise when it comes to music. I think most adults are so glad to see young people attending church that they're willing to turn off their hearing aids or plug their ears with cotton while they endure the contemporary church's joyful music.

There's room for all kinds of music in the church, as long as it glorifies God. Music isn't melodic and harmonious if it takes discord

Forgiveness: The Key to Harmony in the Church

to produce it. Music should bind us together in our fellowship and worship.

We are admonished in the Scriptures to "Make a joyful noise unto the LORD, all ye lands. Serve the LORD with gladness: come before his presence with singing" (Ps. 100:1–2 KJV) and "Talk with each other much about the Lord, quoting psalms and hymns and singing sacred songs, making music in your hearts to the Lord" (Eph. 5:19 TLB). There are lots of scriptures in both the Old and New Testaments that emphasize music as an important part of our worship and praise to God's glory.

We are glad to expand our musical horizon in the church with the choruses of today, but we also want our grandchildren to learn the cherished hymns of yesterday.

Whether the issue dividing the church is great or small, dealing with it requires Christian virtue: "Be humble and gentle. Be patient with each other, making allowance for each other's faults because of your love. Try always to be led along together by the Holy Spirit and so be at peace with one another" (Eph. 4:2–3 TLB).

Paul, in writing to the Corinthian church, deals firmly with issues of divisiveness, immorality, lawsuits, selfishness, abuses of the Lord's Supper, spiritual gifts, and denials of the resurrection. He has a strong message of correction for the Corinthians and for other churches.

He rebukes the Corinthian church for failing to deal with immorality among their members. He makes it clear that he isn't talking about unbelievers who are involved in sexual sins, but those who claim to be Christians. He says you would need to leave this world to avoid people who indulge in blatant sins.

The apostle goes on to say, "It isn't my responsibility to judge outsiders, but it certainly is your responsibility to judge those inside the church who are sinning. God will judge those on the outside; but as the Scriptures say, 'You must remove the evil person from among you'" (1 Cor. 5:12–13 NLT).

Forgiveness: The Key to Lasting Joy

In 2 Corinthians, he writes to the same church, commending them for the actions they have taken. However, he says now it is time to comfort and forgive the man who has sinned so he will be able to recover and know that he's loved.

Paul was demonstrating the kind of concern all of us should model. Mere condemnation should never be our goal when there is a rift in the home or in the church. Restoration is the motive at the heart of true Christianity.

Paul always began his letters with reference to what was positive and good. He expressed God's love for sinners as well as his love for his brothers and sisters in Christ. He ended his letters with an expression of his love and a benediction of God's love for them through Christ.

In working out problems in the church, we need to remember: "Let all that you do be done in love" (1 Cor. 16:14 NASB). We need to treat others with kindness and respect. The church needs to provide a wide open door for forgiveness and reconciliation. The goal of correction and discipline is restoration.

There are those people in the church and in the workplace who say whatever they think. They're often proud of the fact that they're outspoken and boast that they speak their mind. Is that a good thing? I'm inclined to think that if it isn't kind or constructive, it shouldn't be said. If your convictions tell you that you must say something, remember, "The wisdom from above is first of all pure. It is also peace loving, gentle at all times, and willing to yield to others. It is full of mercy and good deeds. It shows no favoritism and is always sincere. And those who are peacemakers will plant seeds of peace and reap a harvest of righteousness" (James 3:17–18 NLT).

We've all known that one person who can't participate in any group discussion without making sparks fly. People like that seem to thrive on strife and conflict. Being argumentative becomes a pattern of behavior for them.

Forgiveness: The Key to Harmony in the Church

Sometimes groups of preachers become engaged in heated discussions and become a bit dogmatic and argumentative. In such a case, the most powerful rebuttal is silence.

Roland was attending a ministers' meeting where they were discussing a controversial subject. One after another, his colleagues voiced their positions. Although the issue was of very little theological significance, the conversation became heated. Once a minister expressed an opinion, he felt compelled to defend his point of view, regardless of the logic from the opposition.

Noting Roland's conspicuous silence, someone turned to him and said, "Roland, you've been very quiet throughout this controversy. What do you think?"

Without hesitation Roland quoted, "Even fools are thought to be wise if they keep silent, and discerning if they hold their tongues" (Prov. 17:28 NIV). The ministers had a good laugh and the camaraderie was restored.

Good-natured disagreements can have a positive effect on the participants. Brainstorming for solutions can often solve problems; however, we've all seen instances when one disagreeable individual can disrupt a meeting. It happens in the business world, at city council meetings, and at school faculty meetings, but it is most troublesome when an individual stirs up strife in a church. In fact, this is one of the seven things that the Lord hates: "one who spreads strife among brothers" (Prov. 6:19b NASB).

By contrast, Barnabas, whose very name means "son of encouragement," blessed the early church. Everything we read about him is positive—he was a good man and full of the Holy Spirit. The book of Acts records that he had a large tract of property, which he sold. He brought the proceeds to the apostles. He then persuaded the Jerusalem church to receive Paul when others did not trust the man who had been the church's chief persecutor. He accompanied Paul on his first missionary journey. Everything we read about him seems to be a commentary on his name, which translates to "son of encouragement."

Everyone needs an encourager. I have been blessed by an aunt who has always been a source of encouragement in my life. Her

Forgiveness: The Key to Lasting Joy

name is Irene, but I call her Aunt Encourager. It was she who led me to the Lord, and she has continued to be a source of spiritual blessing throughout my life. She is now ninety years old, and she still continues her ministry of encouraging others. Every family and every individual needs an encourager in his or her life. Every Christian should be an encourager.

When we began our ministry as a young pastor and his bride, there were those who encouraged us at every step. We thank God for the encouragers He provided at every step of our spiritual journey.

Young people, those who are Christians and those who have not yet come to know the Lord, need encouragement. Our church in Colorado had an abundance of young people. Most of our members rejoiced over our great youth program and gladly invested resources into promoting it. There were a few people, however, who were very critical of the fact that the young people were always at the church playing basketball, having pizza parties, keeping the lights on, and making messes. True, the building might have been cleaner and the electric bill lower if the church facilities sat vacant all week, but where would these young people have gone to find their friends, their recreation, and their Bible studies?

The community's young people, many whose parents had never taken them to church, came for the music, sports activities, and friends they found at the church. It was these programs that brought them to faith in Christ. A large number of our youth are now raising their families in Crossroads Church, while others are serving the Lord throughout our country and even around the world. Roland had the privilege of marrying many of these young people, dedicating their babies, and baptizing their children.

Music has played an important role in our church. We had choirs for every age group from cherub to adult, as well as quartets and trios. The term "Upward Bound" had significance for our members because it was the name of our youth choir that traveled to distant places every year in ministry. The group will never forget the time they were invited to perform at the Baptist World Youth Conference in the Philippines and then went on to sing and share their testimonies in various places in Asia. They also sang at

Forgiveness: The Key to Harmony in the Church

numerous denominational meetings around our country. Every year our youth directors would train the choirs of different age groups and arrange the destinations where the young people could share their faith and proclaim their love for the Lord through music.

The congregation encouraged the young people with their prayers and funds. There were always volunteers to be their sponsors and chaperones when they came up with new ideas to expand their outreach. They stood with the young people in their desire to share their witness when other adults sometimes doubted the wisdom of their proposed adventures.

When Paul was critical of young John Mark, it was Barnabas who came to his defense. He saw his potential rather than his immaturity, and encouraged and mentored him as he took him along on a missionary journey. To his credit, Paul recognized he was wrong; and there was forgiveness and reconciliation between the apostle and this young believer. In a letter to Timothy, Paul paid John Mark a compliment when he wrote, "Get Mark and bring him with you, for he is useful to me for ministry" (2 Tim. 4:11).

There are many young people in our churches today who are eager to be used by our Lord in service and ministry, but they need encouragement from people like Barnabas. Thankfully, there are many of these individuals in our churches.

Some adults in the church, and even parents, can be too critical of young people and discourage them. Some of the things we criticize are insignificant in the Lord's overall plan and purpose. The length of their hair or the style of their clothing needs to be overlooked. The important thing isn't how our children dress when they attend church, but that they go to church. Who are we to criticize the fashions of today? Who looks more ridiculous: the casually dressed young person of this generation or the overdressed lady of my generation? We thought we were quite elegant in our matching hats, gloves, shoes, and purses. We were convinced that we were very stylish with a poodle on our circle skirt and a penny in our shoe. Maybe mismatched hoodies and five layers of shirts aren't so strange after all.

Forgiveness: The Key to Lasting Joy

Perhaps someday we'll reach a happy medium and won't think we have to be too gussied up or too casual. Church should not be about what we wear. It should be about worship and fellowship.

Divisions and quarrels in the church are very hurtful to the cause of Christ. Yes, people are people and Christians are forgiven, not perfect, but we, as the body of Christ, are especially disappointed when a church leader yields to temptation and becomes a major news story. In our disappointment we must remember and proclaim that Christ remains sinless and He is our example. We have no complaint against Him.

There are cases where church boards overstep their authority and use petty, insignificant differences to remove a pastor. One minister accepted the call to a church and moved his family halfway across the country. After two years of successful ministry, one board member decided he didn't like the pastor's style of leadership and persuaded other board members to join him in asking for his resignation.

The pastor could have brought the matter before the congregation and undoubtedly would have prevailed, but he felt the church would be split and the cost of the Christian witness in the community would be too great. Although hurt and disappointed, this strong man of God chose to resign.

A church body should certainly remove a pastor for immorality, but leadership style is not sufficient grounds for dismissal. Some power-hungry laymen need to seek God's forgiveness and the forgiveness of the minister and his family.

In all our years of ministry we never had a church split. We have had serious differences of opinion with some members at times, and a few of them have chosen to find a different church home.

One church member was asked, "Have you had any recent additions to your church?"

He replied, "No, but we've had some blessed subtractions."

Forgiveness: The Key to Harmony in the Church

This is known as a back-door revival. Sometimes such subtractions are a prerequisite to additions and church growth. We tried never to hold any resentment against anyone who left our church.

There are times when we really don't want to forgive. We say to ourselves that our adversary doesn't deserve to be forgiven. We seem to take pleasure in carrying a grudge. We cling to our righteous anger, which is really self-righteous anger. There is something in our nature that keeps us from admitting our wrong and asking for forgiveness.

What keeps me (you) from forgiving others?

- *Stubbornness?*
- *Pride?*
- *Self-righteousness?*
- *Fear of rejection?*
- *Anger?*
- *Bitterness?*

How about thoughts like the following?

- *It's not my fault.*
- *Others are to blame.*
- *They don't deserve forgiveness.*
- *Consider the source.*
- *They've hurt me before.*
- *They're not sincere.*
- *They've hurt me too much.*
- *They never apologize.*
- *They won't accept my apology.*

We're sure you can find other excuses to add to this list, but the truth is, you cannot come up with a reason good enough to ignore your responsibility to forgive.

When we pray the Lord's Prayer, we ask God to "forgive us our trespasses as we forgive those who trespass against us." Whether

Forgiveness: The Key to Lasting Joy

we call our failures trespasses, debts, or sin, do we really want God to forgive us at the same level we forgive others?

An unforgiving heart can form a barrier between us and another church member, or our family and friends. It can also form a barrier between God and us. When you read a scripture or hear a sermon about forgiveness, does it make you feel uncomfortable? Is the Holy Spirit pricking your conscience? Does God bring to your mind a person whom you have failed to forgive? At such a time we are admonished to take action.

The Bible reminds us that inaction is not an option: "If you are standing before the altar in the Temple, offering a sacrifice to God, and suddenly remember that a friend has something against you, leave your sacrifice there beside the altar and go and apologize and be reconciled to him" (Matt. 5:23–24 TLB). This scripture tells us that reconciliation should take precedence over church attendance, taking Communion, giving our tithes and offerings, and charitable work. A prompt apology is of high priority to God. The longer you postpone the apology, the harder it will be.

It might be unwise to apologize to someone who doesn't know that you've gossiped or had unkind thoughts about him or her. You will open a rift that the other person didn't know existed. In such cases, don't go to that individual, go to God. Tell Him you're sorry and then stop the gossip. Go out of your way to befriend the one you've wronged. You'll find that "fire goes out without wood, and quarrels disappear when gossip stops" (Prov. 26:20 NLT).

The church's work would progress far more smoothly if we would look for the best in people and take opportunities to offer sincere compliments where they are deserved.

There's a story about a man who wanted to compliment his minister. He said, "Pastor, your life is so interesting that it should be published."

The pastor responded with characteristic modesty, "Perhaps that can be written posthumously."

With enthusiasm the man replied, "I hope that will be very soon."

Forgiveness: The Key to Harmony in the Church

The church fulfills many of our individual and community needs. It strengthens our faith, and it provides opportunity for service and Christian growth. No one ever needs to be lonely when part of a caring congregation's fellowship. The church shares its people's burdens and sorrows and carries their needs to God in prayer.

The church is the best place to make friends and to find opportunities to serve others. For both children and adults, it is the best place to develop talents and abilities for a lifetime of Christian service. It's the best place to find a spouse. It's also the best place to receive encouragement and to learn how to encourage others.

One of the church's missions is to prepare Christians to serve the Lord. We are instructed, "And let us consider how we may spur one another on toward love and good deeds" (Heb. 10:24 NIV). The church inspires service.

A number of years ago, Connie Zimmerman went to her pastor, my husband, with her burden for helping the poor and homeless. He recognized that this was a concern and passion from God, and he encouraged her to pursue her unique plan to help those in need.

She asked me to serve on her organizing board. With no money—but with prayer and enthusiasm—she began her ministry. Today, after twenty-five years, this nonprofit transitional housing program serves families with children who are classified as "new poor" (families who are homeless for the first time) or "working poor" (families who earn low wages and cannot keep up with the rising cost of living, including housing). Colorado Homeless Families serves approximately forty-seven to seventy-two families annually, with a daily residential population of some 240 to 360 individuals. Their goal is to help people become self-sufficient within eighteen months to two years.

Of course, Connie didn't do all of this by herself, but God used her to challenge others. For example, our daughter-in-law, who is a busy mother and math teacher, donates her time to serve as a board member and secretary to this thriving charity. We are grateful for our children and grandchildren, who have opened their hearts to serving the poor through their churches. They're actively involved in donating to and working in food banks and serving meals to the hungry.

Through the local church our son Jim, and his wife, Terri, opened their home and hearts to a girl from Nepal. Promise lived with them through her senior year of high school, and she became part of the family. Our children and grandchildren were a very positive influence for her at a difficult time in her life. She in turn enriched their lives and broadened their cultural awareness.

I could continue on with many other opportunities for Christian service that have been made available to our children and grandchildren in Colorado, Tennessee, and California because of their church affiliation.

We love the church. We thank God for the wonderful Christian people we have been privileged to serve as pastor and wife. We continue to believe that the friendships made in the church are the most meaningful and lasting ties that bind people together.

Roland was often invited to present his slide and song programs at different churches. One of these engagements took him to the NYNO class banquet. The dinner was held in the social hall of a beautiful, old downtown church. The people were obviously senior citizens. When he asked the meaning of their unique name, he was told NYNO stood for "Not Young, Not Old." The class was originally called the Young Married Couples. They didn't want to be known as the Old Married Class because they were definitely young in spirit. These friends had maintained their close ties for decades, and their bond of fellowship had grown stronger as the years had come and gone.

The ideal church is far more than a sanctuary where people gather on a Sunday morning to hear a sermon and sing praises to God. It's a place where people are equipped to grow in their faith, and where they learn to minister to the poor and impact the community and world for Jesus Christ.

Forgiveness: The Key to Harmony in the Church

My husband and I tend to look at the church through rose-colored glasses because of our personal positive experiences. We wanted to tell only positive things about the church in this book, but that would be less than honest. Yes, the church has sometimes failed. The church is not perfect because it is comprised of imperfect people.

The difference between those on the outside criticizing the church and those of us on the inside is that we recognize we are sinners and need our Savior. Those on the outside do not see their need. As Christians we see our weaknesses and we want to correct them. We help make the church better by becoming more loving, more caring, more forgiving, and more Christlike.

The church is especially helpful as a place for friendship and instruction for new Christians. When I became a Christian I was eager to know everything the Lord wanted me to do. I had never heard of tithing; in fact, I didn't even know how to pronounce the word. I remember being sorry that it was several months before I realized I should give the Lord a tithe, or 10 percent, of what I earned working in the soda fountain.

Christians never outgrow their need for the instruction and fellowship the church provides. They continue to be blessed by worshiping God with other believers as He asks us to do.

There's a story of a mother who said, "I met my husband in church and we were married in the church. We continued to attend the services, and when our first son was able to walk into the church he would go hand in hand with his father. As our family began to grow, it became much easier for us to drop our boy at church and pick him up at the conclusion of the hour.

"One Sunday morning when he was about seven years old, we were seated at the breakfast table. I noticed that he seemed lost in thought, and I wondered what he was thinking.

"My husband also noticed the serious expression on his face and asked, 'Son, what are you thinking about?'

"We were both startled by his response. 'Daddy, don't you love Jesus anymore?'

"His dad replied, 'Of course I do, whatever makes you ask that?'

Forgiveness: The Key to Lasting Joy

"'Well, you don't go to church anymore. My teacher says that if we love Jesus, we will do the things He asks us to do. He asks us to go to church, but you don't go anymore. You used to go with me, and everyone would shake your hand, and say hello, and I felt so happy to be with you. Don't you love Jesus anymore?'

"My husband replied with a husky voice, 'Wait just ten minutes, and I'll be ready to go with you, not just for today, but for always. Today we are a church-going family, and we truly love Jesus.'"

While we recognize that the church is people, we cannot overlook the importance of the church building. Whether the building is humble or grand, whether congregation members built it or an outstanding architect and contractor constructed it, it gives silent witness to the dedication of the members of the body of Christ who meet there. Its care should reflect the church members' devotion. When the building becomes dilapidated and in need of painting and repair, it is a bad reflection on the congregation's commitment. When the building is lovingly cared for by the gifts and labor of God's people, it demonstrates the respect the members have for their place of worship.

In our twenty-nine years of ministry at the Colorado church, we were constantly building, not because we needed to make the edifice more beautiful, but because, even with the addition of multiple services, we needed to make room for our growing congregation. A church's growing pains are desirable because they indicate we are reaching more people for Jesus Christ.

We are happy to say that our church helped sponsor and build churches in our own country and in other places throughout the world. We helped build a church in Nagaland, and another one in Cartagena, Colombia, which we recently visited. Our church also helped fund several church extension projects.

Our son Jim was part of a team from our church that assisted in a building project in Mali, Africa. The people of that congregation formed handmade mud bricks, and with the help of our mission team they added space for their local ministry's expansion.

Forgiveness: The Key to Harmony in the Church

The oldest church in Beaumont, California, is a beautiful stone structure. Years ago members and friends of that church gathered rocks from Whitewater Wash, a number of miles away, and lovingly built the church by hand.

Whether the church is a thatched-roof building in the tropics or a log structure in the Arctic, when the cross is visible it is identified as a Christian church.

We were attracted to a cross on the roof of a humble little building in the Yucatan Peninsula. We joined with a small group of believers and, despite our limited understanding of Spanish, we were blessed by worshiping the Lord with them. We also recall a time when we were in the northern part of Quebec, Canada, and were guided to a great cathedral by its tall steeple with towering cross. Although we didn't understand French, we were able to join with the believers there in worship of the Lord. In spite of language barriers, there's an indescribable oneness with the worldwide family of believers.

We like to picture God's people seated at a Communion table that stretches around the world. Christians of every tribe, race, and language partake together of the emblems that represent the broken body and the shed blood of our Lord Jesus Christ. It is He Himself who invites everyone to come to Him and to His table. He wants everyone to receive forgiveness and eternal life.

What is the church? The church is people—forgiven people.

Your Turn

1. What are some of the excuses people use for not attending church?

2. How can I help maintain or restore harmony in my church? Am I intergenerational in my support of changes in church music and activities or do I consider only what my generation likes?

Forgiveness: The Key to Lasting Joy

3. When I pray the Lord's Prayer, am I sincere in praying, "Forgive us our debts as we forgive our debtors"? Does God bring someone to mind that I need to forgive?

4

Forgiveness: The Key to Surviving Tragedy

WE SINCERELY HOPE that your family or someone you know has not had to endure the death of a child, or been the victim of an accident, crime, life-threatening illness, or the loss of a loved one in war. The hard truth is that there is no home in the land that has not felt this hush.

The bitter question comes: "Where is God in our times of tragedy?" Of course, this question will never be answered to our complete satisfaction this side of heaven.

I've been with my husband when we've tried to comfort parents who've lost a child. Roland has had the sad experience of conducting many children's funerals. There is no adequate comfort for grieving parents from friends, families, or ministers, yet we try to offer words of encouragement as we weep with those who weep. Even Jesus wept with Mary and Martha at the death of their brother Lazarus.

The Bible gives us three ways in which to deal with the burdens of life. The first is, "Every man shall bear his own burden" (Gal. 6:5 KJV). This is a very lonely method of dealing with life's tragedies. The second is, "Bear ye one another's burdens, and so fulfil the law of Christ" (Gal. 6:2 KJV). Our burdens are lighter when others help us carry them. The third and best way to deal with the burdens

Forgiveness: The Key to Lasting Joy

of life is to "cast thy burden upon the LORD, and he shall sustain thee" (Ps. 55:22a KJV).

Dr. Oswald J. Smith, the great preacher from Canada, wrote words of comfort for his sister Ruth when she lost her missionary husband in an accident in Peru. He wrote:

> God understands your sorrow
> He sees the falling tear,
> And whispers, "I am with thee."
> Then falter not, nor fear.
>
> He understands your heartache
> Your deepest grief he shares.
> Then let him bear your burden.
> He understands and cares.

Dana Smith was an outstanding athlete as a child and in high school, where she broke records in swimming, basketball, track, and volleyball. In Dana's scrapbook is a letter of intent offer for a full athletic scholarship to Stanford University. It was the first full athletic scholarship Stanford ever offered to a female athlete. She chose, however, an all-expenses-paid volleyball scholarship to the University of Southern California.

We recently attended an awards ceremony for Dana at USC in the new Galen Center. While the band played, a huge banner hanging from the ceiling was uncovered with the name "Dana Smith Casey" and her jersey, number 4, printed in bold letters. She was honored as a USC women's volleyball "All Time Great." While at USC, Dana was an All-American three years in succession, a two-time national champion, an NCAA postgraduate scholarship winner, and a Top Ten Scholar Athlete award winner.

After graduation from the university, Dana became a volleyball coach and teacher. She married her high school sweetheart and they had two children. Their storybook life was interrupted by a new

Forgiveness: The Key to Surviving Tragedy

challenge, greater than any that Dana had faced on the volleyball court, when she was diagnosed with stage-4 breast cancer.

In her dilemma over where and how she should seek treatment, her husband, Richard, discovered a special Bible verse: "Trust in the LORD with all your heart, and lean not on your own understanding. In all your ways acknowledge Him, and He shall direct your paths" (Prov. 3:5–6).

Following this biblical promise, they felt led to the City of Hope, where she underwent surgery and months of treatment. She had stem cell replacement therapy, a new procedure that harvests the patient's stem cells and subsequently replaces them in his or her body.

After months of treatment and much prayer, Dana was able to return to her busy life and could once again attend her son's football games. Andrew was in his senior year of high school, and his accomplishments brought him many offers of possible athletic scholarships from prestigious universities across the country.

One evening Dana was seated on the bleachers, thanking God for her returned health and the joy of watching her son play football. She was praying for Andrew and for his teammates. She said she had never felt so close to God before. Then the unthinkable happened: Andrew was hit hard while making a tackle and didn't get up.

As Dana rushed to his side, she could see that his leg was broken. She watched in horror as her son writhed in pain there on the playing field. Obviously, his season was over and his hopes for a football scholarship were gone. In anger and disappointment, she asked God, "Why did You let this happen just as I was praying for Andrew and I felt so close to You?"

It didn't take God long to answer her question. While the physicians were preparing to operate on Andrew's leg, they discovered that he had a rare, life-threatening heart defect, the type that has taken the life of so many promising athletes who seem to be in perfect health.

Not knowing where to go for diagnosis and treatment, the family turned to God and drew on the wisdom of their special verse, Proverbs 3:5–6. God directed their path and Andrew was referred to a renowned heart surgeon at the University of Southern California Medical Center. He was able to detect a very dangerous abnormality with technology that only recently had been developed.

This famous cardiologist performed a rare and delicate operation that saved Andrew's life. Even with the doctor's vast experience, it was only the fifth operation of this kind he had ever performed.

At the very time Dana was seated on the bleachers praying for Andrew and was feeling so close to God, her heavenly Father was demonstrating His great unfailing love. He permitted Andrew to break his leg to save his life.

We recently attended a hard-fought college football game where we sat on the bleachers with Andrew's parents, grandparents, and a group of enthusiastic supporters watching him play. We cheered and thanked God for Andrew's broken leg (now healed) and for his life-saving heart surgery.

We don't know why God saved Andrew's life and not Tommy's, Mark's, Spencer's, or your child's life, but we do know God loves you. As Oswald Smith wrote, "God understands your heartache, your deepest grief He shares.... God understands and cares."

We've often heard people say, "I'm angry with God. How could He let this happen?" Does God leave us when we turn away from Him? No, even when our faith is weak, He is faithful and He continues to love us. God recognizes that our vision is limited. We see only the immediate. He sees the big picture.

My sisters and my nieces have experienced the great sorrow that comes with the loss of a child or a grandchild. In our family's shared grief we tried to comfort each other, but the real comfort came from our loving heavenly Father.

We were traveling on Interstate 70 in eastern Colorado when we were surprised by an early spring blizzard. In the whiteout conditions, my niece Sherry and I lost sight of my husband following us in the used RV he was transporting to a relative.

After miles of white-knuckle driving, we reached a freeway exit. We were confident Roland couldn't miss it because the road ahead was closed and traffic was diverted. The little café where we took refuge was soon filled with frustrated travelers. As we waited

Forgiveness: The Key to Surviving Tragedy

for Roland and listened to accounts of accidents and cars stuck in snow banks, our anxiety mounted.

At last a police car drove up and out stepped my husband, shaken but uninjured. The camper had slid off the icy road onto its side. A tow truck was called to take it to a garage.

The motels in the small town of Flagler were completely filled and we were trying to prepare ourselves for a cold and miserable night in the damaged RV when a local church's pastor arrived. He was an angel of mercy out in the blizzard, looking for stranded travelers. He explained that it wasn't unusual for people in his little town and other towns in eastern Colorado and western Kansas to open their homes to shelter strangers in distress.

At the pastor's invitation, we climbed into his four-wheel-drive vehicle. He deposited us at his home and into his wife's care before going out again.

The storm continued, but in the warmth of their welcome, it was almost forgotten. Conversation came easy and we found we had lots in common.

The next morning Roland and I were told that the pastor and his wife shared a deep sorrow with my niece. They had both lost a young son. After we went to bed, Sherry and our hostess had stayed up most of the night talking. My first thought was how wonderful it was that the pastor's wife had been able to comfort and help Sherry. To my surprise, she told us how God had used Sherry to comfort her. In truth, they comforted each other. They were snow angels brought together by a closed road and our loving God's providence.

For an unbeliever, a child's death certainly would leave parents in despair for the rest of their lives. Life would be meaningless. In the Christian worldview, however, we have the assurance that the day is coming when everything will be made right and the dreaded enemy—death—will be destroyed. As Christians, we know our future is as bright as God's promises and that we will see our loved ones again.

In his book *Man's Search for Meaning*, Viktor E. Frankl reminds us that meaning for life is found in a biblical worldview, which says, "We have been made by God and for God."

Forgiveness: The Key to Lasting Joy

The Bible says, "For by Him all things were created, both in the heavens and on earth, visible and invisible, whether thrones or dominions or rulers or authorities—all things have been created through Him and for Him. He is before all things, and in Him all things hold together" (Col. 1:16–17 NASB).

When we recognize that God is God, and His purposes are eternal, we are able to accept that our view is limited and we can trust Him with our loved ones and our lives.

On a recent Amtrak trip Roland helped a man who walked with the aid of a crutch and a cane. He and his wife were loaded down with an excessive amount of luggage. The couple said they were accustomed to traveling with lots of baggage because when their little boy was alive he required a special wheelchair.

I said, "I'm sorry. How long has it been since you lost your little boy?"

"Almost a year," the man answered. Then they showed us a scrapbook page with four photos of their son. In each picture, the first thing that caught our eyes was the radiant smile that spread across the boy's face. His little body was strapped into his wheelchair, but his face was that of a truly free spirit.

The man explained that their son's life expectancy was thirteen years, but they were blessed to have him for twenty-six years. He said his wife should have had a cesarean section when the baby was born but the doctor failed to perform the procedure. Their son began his life with multiple physical difficulties and never grew beyond the size of a small boy. He was never able to walk.

This couple showed no bitterness toward the doctor or toward God. If they ever had had difficulty forgiving their physician, they certainly had overcome their resentment. They saw their little baby boy who never grew up as their special gift from God. Their eyes sparkled as they said, "Our son is now running and skipping around heaven. We look forward to seeing him again in God's good time."

What part does forgiveness play in enabling people to turn unspeakable tragedy into something of great benefit and blessing to hundreds of hurting people?

Forgiveness: The Key to Surviving Tragedy

Carol Ragan, the beautiful daughter of James and Arlene Ragan, was an excellent teacher who was involved in many community organizations to help children. In 1996 she was struck and killed by a drunk driver. The last words in her private journal were, "Ask your heart what is right and follow it."

How could Carol's grieving parents ever move beyond their anguish? Forgiving the drunk driver and even forgiving God must have seemed impossible to them, but in the midst of their grief, they took a step of faith.

Inspired by Carol's philosophy of giving and caring for others, her parents founded Carol's Kitchen. On April 21, 1998, Carol's Kitchen opened its doors for the first time and fed thirty-four hungry men, women, and children.

Today, Carol's Kitchen serves more than 150,000 meals per year in five separate San Gorgonio Pass locations in Southern California. More than two hundred volunteers welcome and serve God's hungry children.

James and Arlene made a beautiful choice to let good grow out of grief. Perhaps forgiveness and healing is something that comes when we move beyond our own personal tragedy to respond to the needs of other hurting people. No one would have blamed the Ragans if they had continued on in their grief and even in self-pity, but that wouldn't have helped them or anyone else. By choosing to help others, they also helped themselves.

Amy Biehl was an outstanding student at Stanford University. Driven by her concern over the injustice of apartheid in South Africa, she chose to continue her studies at the University of the Western Cape in Cape Town with the Fulbright Scholar Program.

In 1993 Amy drove a friend to her home in the township of Gugulethu outside of Cape Town. A black mob attacked the white woman's car, shouting racial epithets. They smashed the windows, dragged her from her car, stoned her, and stabbed her to death.

Four men were convicted and imprisoned for the murder. In 1998, several years after the end of apartheid, and with Amy's parents' support, all four were pardoned.

Forgiveness: The Key to Lasting Joy

Amy's father shook his daughter's killer's hand. He said, "The most important vehicle of reconciliation is open and honest dialogue.... We are here to reconcile a human life which was taken without an opportunity for dialogue. When we are finished with this process, we must move forward with linked arms."

These exceptional parents established the Amy Biehl Foundation Trust to empower young people in the township to work to discourage further violence. Amy's legacy lives on in the United States and South Africa. It is especially evident in the changed lives of Ntobeko Peni and Easy Nofemela, two of the men who were participants in her murder. Today they are transformed men who work for that which is just and good.

We might see how someone could forgive an accident, but not a deliberate crime. The story of Amy Biehl's murder was a purposeful and heinous act of brutality. Her parents chose to forgive rather than perpetuate the hatred and racism that had ripped apart the entire country of South Africa. Amy's life and death contributed to the defeat of apartheid and validated her personal dedication and that of her parents to the cause of racial justice and forgiveness.

On May 13, 1981, the world was shocked by an assassination attempt on Pope John Paul II. He was shot four times and critically wounded in St. Peter's Square in Vatican City. Mehmet Ali Agca, from Turkey, was arrested and later sentenced to life in prison by an Italian court.

Pope John Paul II asked people to pray for Agca, and said he had already forgiven him. In 1983 the two met and spoke privately at the prison where Agca was held. Agca was released from prison in January 2010.

We remember the Roman Catholic Youth Rally held in Denver at the Cherry Creek State Park on August 15, 1993. Pope John Paul II addressed the great gathering. Protestants and Catholics embraced his message because he lived the compassion and forgiveness he preached.

Forgiveness: The Key to Surviving Tragedy

When Roland and I, along with our daughter, toured the Auschwitz concentration camp in Poland, we were horrified by what we saw. It brought to mind the story of Corrie ten Boom.

Corrie was a Dutch Christian Holocaust survivor. She and her family helped many Jews escape from the Nazis during World War II. Her autobiography, *The Hiding Place,* and the subsequent movie by the same title depict her life and the horrors of imprisonment in a German concentration camp.

In 1942, before being taken to the camp, Corrie and her family were active in the Dutch Underground. They rescued Jews from certain death at the hands of the Nazi Secret Service, hiding them and other members of the Dutch Resistance in a room designed by a sympathetic architect. The Nazis never found this room; it was the perfect hiding place.

The Germans arrested the entire ten Boom family in 1944. They were taken to Scheveningen Prison, where Corrie's father died. Some members of her family were released, but Corrie and her sister, Betsie, were sent to Vught Concentration Camp and finally to the infamous Ravensbruck in Germany. Conditions were so deplorable and the guards were so brutal that Betsie died. By the miracle of a clerical error, Corrie was mistakenly freed. She later learned that the week following her release, the female prisoners her age were killed.

After the war, Corrie spent her time teaching and writing about God's forgiveness through Christ and about forgiving others. In her book *Tramp for the Lord,* she recalls the incident when, after a speaking engagement in Germany, one of the most cruel Ravensbruck guards approached her. She knew she must forgive him, but how could she? She prayed for God's help. She wrote, "For a long moment we grasped each other's hands, the former guard and the former prisoner. I had never known God's love so intensely as I did then."

Corrie went on to say that of all the people she had known who were victims of Nazi brutality, it was those who were able to forgive who were best able to rebuild their lives.

Forgiveness: The Key to Lasting Joy

When Corrie was asked if she remembered a particularly horrendous event in her life, she replied that she distinctly remembered forgetting that. There are things we must remember to forgive and forget in our lives. The time comes to let it go.

Jesus instructs us to do what seems to be impossible when He asks us to go even beyond forgiving our enemies. These are His words: "I say to you, love your enemies, bless those who curse you, do good to those who hate you, and pray for those who spitefully use you and persecute you" (Matt. 5:44). How can mere human beings leave our hatred behind and progress to loving our enemies? Only with God's grace, with His love and forgiveness in our lives, can we make this love possible.

A remarkable example of this Christian grace comes from the American Revolutionary War period. A man named Wildman, who lived in Ephrata, Pennsylvania, took pleasure in verbally abusing Pastor Peter Miller of the Dunker Church.

Wildman enlisted in the Continental Army. While he was in the service, he was arrested and tried for being a spy. He was convicted and sentenced to be hanged.

Pastor Miller heard about the sentence and walked sixty miles to Philadelphia to intercede for Wildman. When he made his plea to General George Washington, the general replied, "I am sorry, but I cannot grant your request to spare your friend's life."

"But sir, he's not my friend," Miller explained. "He's my worst enemy."

"You mean you walked sixty miles to plead for the life of your enemy? That puts the matter in a different light. Your request is granted."

Washington signed the pardon and gave it to Miller. He walked another fifteen miles to where Wildman was to be executed. When Wildman saw Pastor Miller coming, he said to the other convicts, "There comes old Pete. He came to see me hanged."

Miller made his way through the crowd and gave the condemned man the pardon. Did Wildman ask Miller and God for forgiveness? Did he have a change of heart and become a believer? We don't know, but Pastor Miller put into practice Jesus' teachings to "love your enemies."

Forgiveness: The Key to Surviving Tragedy

Of course we will never find an example that is comparable to that of our Lord Jesus Christ, as He prayed hanging on the cruel cross, "Father, forgive them, for they do not know what they do" (Luke 23:34).

The apostles chose Stephen for a special ministry. His task was to provide food for the widows who were dependent on the early church. He was full of faith and the Holy Spirit's power, and he had a good reputation among the people.

He angered some Jews when he preached about Jesus and accused the religious leaders of murdering the Messiah. The Jewish leaders were enraged by Stephen's accusations and his claim that he could see Jesus standing at God's right hand.

The angry mob dragged Stephen out of the city to be stoned. As the stones were hurled at him, Stephen called out, "Lord Jesus, receive my spirit!" He fell on his knees and cried with a loud voice, "Lord, do not hold this sin against them!" And with that he died, the first Christian martyr.

On December 7, 1941, the Japanese bombed Pearl Harbor in a surprise attack. President Roosevelt called it "a date which will live in infamy."

It was a day of great collective sorrow for our nation, but there was also great personal sorrow for the grieving families who lost their loved ones in that surprise attack. World War II went on to claim 416,800 American casualties, but numbers of casualties don't tell the heartbreaking story of individual lives lost in war. There was a broken heart left behind each father, mother, son, daughter, sister, or brother killed in that great and horrible war.

Does God expect us to forgive our war enemies after we've signed a peace treaty? It doesn't seem possible that God would ask us to forgive those who attacked us so viciously without provocation, but He tells us, "But I say to you who hear: Love your enemies, do good to those who hate you, bless those who curse you, and pray for those who spitefully use you" (Luke 6:27–28). God not only

Forgiveness: The Key to Lasting Joy

asks us to forgive, but He goes to the extreme when He asks us to love our enemies and pray for them.

Captain Mitsuo Fuchida was the bomber pilot who led the attack on Pearl Harbor on that Sunday morning in 1941.

On that same day, Jacob DeShazer was on KP duty at his Army air base in Pendleton, Oregon, when he heard over the loudspeaker that the Japanese had bombed Pearl Harbor. He threw a potato at the wall in unrestrained outrage.

Jacob served as a bombardier on a B-25 under the command of Jimmy Doolittle. He volunteered for a secret bombing raid on Japan. After the successful raid, they ran out of fuel and had to parachute into enemy territory, and were captured the next day.

DeShazer was held in POW camps for forty months. Over half of that time he was in solitary confinement, where he was beaten and nearly starved to death. Three of the crew were executed by a firing squad and one died of starvation.

The Japanese allowed DeShazer to have a Bible for three weeks. In that brief time with God's Word, he became a Christian.

DeShazer was liberated when American soldiers parachuted into the prison camp. After he recuperated, he returned to Japan, and for the next thirty years he shared the message of God's love and forgiveness with his former enemies.

After the war, Captain Fuchida testified before the war crimes tribunal. He was convinced that the Americans were as guilty as the Japanese of cruel treatment of their prisoners. Yet his former flight engineer, who had been a prisoner in an American prison camp, told him that a young lady whose missionary parents had been killed by the Japanese in the Philippines had treated him with love and respect.

In the Bushido code, revenge was required to restore honor. The killers of the young woman's parents should have been her enemies for life, but she chose to forgive them and even to love them.

Fuchida was so amazed by this young Christian woman's forgiveness that he purchased a New Testament. God was working in his heart when he was given a copy of DeShazar's story, *I Was a Prisoner of Japan*. He started to throw it away, but when he saw

Forgiveness: The Key to Surviving Tragedy

that the author was a Doolittle Raider, he read it. He embraced Jesus' words from the cross, "Father, forgive them, for they know not what they do" (Luke 23:34). He became a Christian and was baptized on Easter Sunday 1951.

This Japanese captain became a Christian evangelist. He toured the United States as a member of the Worldwide Christian Missionary Army of Sky Pilots. He spent the rest of his life sharing Christ's love and the story of God's forgiveness with Americans, while Jacob DeShazer devoted his life to sharing the good news of God's forgiveness with the Japanese.

Captain Fuchida, who bombed Pearl Harbor, and Jacob DeShazer, the Doolittle Raider who bombed Japan, became close friends. Only God could accomplish this miracle of forgiveness in the hearts of these once bitter enemies.

God also can bring about forgiveness between nations that were once at war. Some of the United States' most reliable allies are those with whom we have once fought in bitter wars. England, Germany, and Japan are no longer enemies—they are now our friends.

Our most recent and perhaps most dangerous enemy is not a nation, but an ideology. While writing this book on forgiveness we came to the ninth anniversary of 9/11, the day that changed our country forever. We wanted to ignore this event as it relates to forgiveness, but we could not.

The brutal and devastating attack on the Twin Towers, the Pentagon, and the airplane that crashed in Pennsylvania were so horrendous that the very thought of forgiving the perpetrators of that unspeakable crime seemed beyond our ability.

Then God spoke to us over the centuries through His prophet Micah: "What does the LORD require of you but to do justly, to love mercy, and to walk humbly with your God?" (Micah 6:8).

The first requirement in our reaction is to act justly. Justice after 9/11 required retaliation and punishment. We are grateful for our service men and women, along with their families, who continue to sacrifice so much to keep us safe and to prevent such evil from ever being perpetrated against our country again.

Forgiveness: The Key to Lasting Joy

The next divine requirement is to love mercy. Mercy is unmerited favor. The greatest example of mercy was Jesus dying on the cross for our hideous sins. We cannot ignore God's call for us to extend mercy to others.

Jesus adds another requirement: He tells us to love our enemies. How can we love our enemies who want to destroy us and our way of life? We can't begin to understand the terrorist who wants to become a martyr and is ready to claim virtue in dying even while murdering innocent civilians. Our concept of a true martyr comes from the first Christian martyr, Stephen, and his Christlike prayer for his murderers to absolve them of their guilt.

Our final word from Micah is, "Walk humbly with your God." What if we had been born into a Muslim home? What if instead of being taught Jesus' love, we had been taught by a radical Imam and had become a Jihadist? "There but for the grace of God go I."

Maybe this is the time to recall God's message to the whole world, Muslims included: "For God so loved the world, that He gave His only begotten Son, that whoever believes in Him shall not perish, but have eternal life" (John 3:16 NASB).

In the days following the collapse of the Twin Towers, many workmen risked their lives to find and rescue survivors. A number of workers came upon two steel beams in the shape of a twenty-foot cross standing erect in the rubble of 6 World Trade Center's basement. When Frank Silecchia, a man of faith, saw that cross, he stood there and wept. For him those beams were a symbol that represented Jesus, who was lifted up on the cross, descended into the grave, and then rose triumphant over the grave.

Silecchia saw to it that the cross was salvaged and placed where Mass was celebrated at Ground Zero. To Silecchia and many others, the cross spoke of God's love in the midst of unspeakable tragedy.

Paul wrote to the Corinthian Christians, "For the preaching of the cross is to them that perish foolishness; but unto us which are saved it is the power of God" (1 Cor. 1:18 KJV).

Sir John Bowering, former governor of Hong Kong, is said to have visited Macao on the south China coast. He saw a cross on the pinnacle of a wall that once had been a glorious cathedral. A

Forgiveness: The Key to Surviving Tragedy

typhoon left only the great bronze cross standing in the midst of twisted wreckage.

The vision of that cross, elevated above the rubble of the once-proud worship center, made a lasting impression on Bowering's mind, and he wrote the words to the hymn "In the Cross of Christ."

Bowering was a famous biographer, naturalist, financier, statesman, and linguist. His writings include thirty-six volumes of published work. Despite all of his accomplishments, he is known today primarily as the author of this simple hymn, which was engraved on his tombstone and gives silent witness to his faith in Jesus Christ:

> In the Cross of Christ I glory
> Towering o'er the wrecks of time;
> All the light of sacred story
> Gathers round its head sublime.

When tragedy comes, whether it is caused by a natural phenomenon such as a typhoon or by an unspeakable crime committed by terrorists, the cross of Christ is the one symbol that speaks love and forgiveness to all who look with faith to the crucified Lord.

God spoke through the rubble of Ground Zero with the emblem of the cross. He continues to offer hope and healing in the midst of broken lives and broken dreams. To those who looked to the cross at Ground Zero, God seemed to say that He was there and that He would triumph over tragedy. The cross of Christ is the symbol of hope for individuals and for nations.

In his autobiography, *Son of Hamas*, Mosab Hassan Yousef writes about his life as the son of the cofounder of Hamas. He recounts how he went from being part of the terrorist organization to becoming a Christian.

Yousef, who now attends a Baptist church in San Diego, is known to his friends by his English name, Joseph. He has said that real peace between the Palestinian people and Israel is only possible when both sides understand the principles of forgiveness as Jesus taught.

Forgiveness: The Key to Lasting Joy

We've had a recent association with a Muslim whom we sincerely appreciate. Our daughter and son-in-law live next door to Cindy and Mohammad. She is a nurse, and he is a pediatric cardiologist. During a conversation with Cindy, our daughter shared some concerns about her husband's health.

Cindy described Jack's symptoms to her husband and told him she thought he should talk to Jack. Mohammad recognized some serious danger signals and told Jack to get an angiogram. Soon after this conversation, Jack was at school teaching his science class when he felt the dangerous symptoms reoccur. He left school and went directly to the emergency room and was admitted to the hospital.

Immediately after they administered an angiogram, the doctors ordered Jack to be transferred by ambulance to a renowned heart center. Within hours he received a five-way bypass, an open-heart surgery. Today Jack is back teaching and living an active life. We are all thanking God for our Muslim friend who was used as a messenger to save Jack's life.

Shelter Now International (SNI) is a foreign aid organization that serves the poor in Afghanistan. The book and movie *Kabul 24* tell the gripping story of eight aid workers and sixteen Afghan natives who were arrested on August 3, 2001. The Taliban held them hostage as pawns in the political and religious turmoil following 9/11. They were rescued by American Special Forces after 105 days in captivity.

The eight Christian aid workers forgave their captors and some of them were able to return to help the needy in Afghanistan. Today, Shelter Now International's work continues to provide emergency aid, housing, schools, vocational training, and irrigation in Afghanistan and Pakistan. Their story demonstrates loving your enemy in action.

In the midst of tragedy, some people think of God as their enemy. They can't believe that God would permit such calamities to overtake them. Some even shake their fist at God, and in their

Forgiveness: The Key to Surviving Tragedy

anger and self-pity, they reject God's help and comfort. We need to remember that God sees the forever and we see the immediate. When we recognize that God is God and we are at peace with Him, life has real meaning.

Although we never will fully understand God's plans and purposes, we can come to Him by faith and receive His peace and comfort in the midst of our sorrows.

The Bible tells us, "The eternal God is thy refuge, and underneath are the everlasting arms" (Deut. 33:27 KJV). These words were a great source of blessing to Roland's mother because they were her husband's parting message from his hospital bed in Colombia, South America. He knew he was leaving her to raise five children and a sixth on the way. She was in a foreign land, without any relatives within thousands of miles.

Martha Taylor could have become bitter and asked, "Why has God taken my husband just when we are attempting to do His work?" But she turned in faith to the only adequate refuge, and promised her husband that she would raise his children in the "nurture and admonition of the Lord" (Eph. 6:4 KJV).

Martha fulfilled her promise. She lived a life of dedication to her Lord. All of her six children were serving the Lord when she was reunited with her husband.

Roland saw an old family friend a few days after his mom's funeral. The friend said, "Roland, I understand your mother has received her promotion." Her home-going was indeed a promotion. She faithfully fulfilled her promise to her missionary husband and to her Lord.

Many people spend their whole lives fearing death, the death of a loved one or their own death. Fear of the future paralyzes their present. They fear what won't happen and what will happen. They fear growing old and they fear dying young. We need to ask God to forgive us for our doubts and fears and to replace them with faith and trust in His conquering power.

Forgiveness: The Key to Lasting Joy

In 1 Corinthians 15, that great chapter on the resurrection, we are told, "Christ will be King until he has defeated all his enemies, including the last enemy—death" (1 Cor. 15:25–26 TLB). The Bible assures us that the Christian *has* (present possession) eternal life. We do not despair as those who have no hope. So then the question is this: How do we help others in the midst of their despair? The Christian has the privilege and responsibility of sharing the hope of triumph over tragedy through Jesus Christ with those who are hurting. Our greatest comfort is to be found in the Scriptures. Jesus' invitation is, "Come to Me, all who are weary and heavy-laden, and I will give you rest" (Matt. 11:28 NASB). When individuals or nations are distraught in the midst of tragedy, whether it is the death of one child or the loss of thousands of people in an earthquake or tsunami, Christians must make themselves available to provide physical and spiritual assistance.

When the earthquake shook the poverty-stricken country of Haiti, Samaritan's Purse and World Vision, along with countless other Christian organizations, rushed in to help. Through our gifts to such organizations, we partner with them in the name of Christ to alleviate hunger, pain, and suffering.

Compassion International continues to help impoverished children around the world through its child sponsorship program. This ministry began in 1952 to help Korean War orphans, and now more than a million children in twenty-six countries are being helped by caring sponsors. We can't do everything, but we can do something. By sponsoring even one child we can make a difference, one child at a time.

Steve and Debbie, our son and his wife, gave a presentation at their church to help promote the work of Compassion International. The following was Steve's introduction to their challenging message:

> It was our first date, twenty-six years ago. I came to pick up Debbie at her place. She invited me in, and I noticed a photo of a little girl on her refrigerator. I said, "Who's this?" She said, "That's Maritha from Guatemala. She's a child I sponsor through an organization called Compassion. Have you heard of it?" And I

Forgiveness: The Key to Surviving Tragedy

said, "Really? Because I sponsor a child from Compassion." She said, "Really?" I said, "Yeah—a little girl from Malaysia." I felt like proposing to her right then.

Steve and Debbie have continued to sponsor children throughout their marriage. They currently have five whom they have been able to visit in their native lands. Because of their example, we, like others in the family, are now Compassion sponsors.

Christian concern requires that we help people in distant lands and close at home. A hurting neighbor may need our comfort at the death of a loved one. Another may need financial assistance after the loss of a job. We as Christians must respond with love and concern to the physical needs of hurting people, but we must also share the message of eternal hope through Jesus Christ our Lord.

I love being a minister's wife—not just any minister's wife, but Roland's wife. Over the years it has opened up opportunities for me to encourage people in their times of need and sorrow and to help lift their burdens. Somehow a burden becomes lighter when another person helps you carry it. That's why God, through His servant Paul, told us to bear each other's burdens.

I can listen, I can pray with a hurting person, and most of all I can point them to the Lord, who is the real burden-bearer. We are told, "Cast your burden upon the LORD and He will sustain you" (Ps. 55:22 NASB). You can listen and you can pray and point people to the Lord.

We want to comfort those who sorrow. It's true that we can't answer their questions of why they've experienced such tragedy, but we can remind them of God's love and stand with them in their sorrow.

When I'm afraid, I try to remind myself to trust in the Lord. Then I pray, "Help me, Lord, to trust You and not be afraid." The Bible tells us that Jesus' perfect love takes away fear.

It seems almost a natural instinct for us to be concerned about the dangers that can befall our children or grandchildren. An unknown poet wrote the following eulogy to a mother, describing that natural tendency.

Forgiveness: The Key to Lasting Joy

> She always stood and watched for us,
> Anxious if we were late,
> In winter by the window,
> In summer by the gate.
> And though we mocked her tenderly
> Who had such foolish care,
> The long way home would seem more safe
> Because she waited there.
> Her thoughts were all so full of us
> She never would forget
> And now I think that where she is
> She must be waiting yet.
> Waiting till we come home to her,
> Anxious if we are late.
> Watching from Heaven's window
> Leaning from Heaven's gate.

As we grow older, it is natural to be concerned about losing our lifetime companion. Our dear friend, Fern, recently lost her husband of more than fifty-five years. She told me that she found her greatest comfort in praising the Lord. That sounds impossible from a natural standpoint, but she chooses to think about the Lord's mercy and all the treasured memories she has.

After my mother's funeral, we drove home to Colorado from California. We took a detour through Zion National Park. As we were standing on a bridge, looking out at the beauty of God's creation, I commented to my husband, "I wish Mom could see this." Then I laughed as I said, "I can just hear her saying, 'Just wait until they see this!'"

The Bible says, "No mere man has ever seen, heard, or even imagined what wonderful things God has ready for those who love the Lord" (1 Cor. 2:9 TLB). We stand in awe at the beauty of God's creation as we travel throughout the world, but the beauty of heaven surpasses anything we can ever imagine.

You may ask: How does all this talk about heaven relate to the topic of forgiveness, this book's subject? Heaven is all about forgiveness. We are welcomed into heaven because we have received God's forgiveness through our Lord Jesus Christ.

Forgiveness: The Key to Surviving Tragedy

When we think of our own mortality, let's change our focus to our immortality. We don't want to succumb to fear for our loved ones' health and lives or for our own lives, "For God has not given us a spirit of fear, but of power and of love and of a sound mind" (2 Tim. 1:7). Fear doesn't come from God; He gives hope and assurance of heaven. Without God, man is without hope. There certainly is much of which to be afraid in our world today. Those who deny God's existence have reason to be afraid. After all, where does an unbeliever turn for comfort when he is afraid?

We can deny God's existence or we can turn to Him in faith. There are two ways to respond to tragedy: fatalism or faith. We can become bitter and hardened and resolve to conquer on our own, or we can trust in God.

Our world is fragile. Our lives are fragile. We can take comfort in the fact that we are held in God's steady hands, and the knowledge that we are forgiven. Our forgiveness is secure because it is not based on what we do, but on what Christ did when He died on the cross to forgive our sins.

Your Turn

1. Do you know someone who has been able to forgive the seemingly unforgivable? How were they able to do this?

2. How have you been able to cope with tragedy in your life? Have tragic events brought you closer to God, or alienated you from Him?

3. When is anger justified? When you recognize that anger fails to bring comfort, how can you move forward with your life?

5

Forgiveness: The Key to Heaven

WHAT DO YOU need? What do you want and desire more than anything else? I know what I want: life. I'm quite certain that if you could choose any gift your heart desires, you would choose life too.

God offers this greatest of all gifts—the gift of eternal life—to you and to me. It's exactly what we need. It is of inestimable value because it will last forever.

The angel of the Lord announced the wonderful news of the arrival of God's gift about two thousand years ago, but the news is still as exciting today as it was on that night so long ago. It was spoken to a group of shepherds on a hillside near Bethlehem, but it was intended for all people throughout the whole world. It was great news then and it continues to be great news for all generations since that time. The angel declared, "I bring you the most joyful news ever announced, and it is for everyone! The Savior—yes, the Messiah, the Lord—has been born tonight in Bethlehem!" (Luke 2:10b–11 TLB).

Even if we searched all the sophisticated news sources of our day, we wouldn't be able to find a single announcement that compares with the importance of the news those shepherds heard on that first Christmas night. It was God's way of announcing the

Forgiveness: The Key to Lasting Joy

gift of His one and only Son to the world: "God showed how much he loved us by sending his only Son into this wicked world to bring to us eternal life through his death. In this act we see what real love is: it is not our love for God but his love for us when he sent his Son to satisfy God's anger against our sins" (1 John 4:9–10 TLB).

People don't like to confront the question of sin. It is sometimes called a mistake, an error in judgment, or any term that fails to clearly define man's evil heart or his rebellious acts and intents. In reality, sin is any departure from God's known will.

Let's say I have a bottle of poison in my medicine cabinet with an ugly skull and crossbones on the label, and the word *poison* clearly displayed. If I substitute a bouquet of roses for the skull and crossbones or change the disagreeable word *poison* to *essence of peppermint,* I don't remove the danger of its contents. The less obnoxious the label appears, the more dangerous the bottle becomes. In the same way, the more we dilute the terms we apply to man's rebellion against God, the greater is the danger that we will reap the whirlwind of God's wrath against sinful man's evil thoughts and actions.

We need God's pardon provided by His sinless Son to atone for our sins. God's forgiveness through Jesus Christ is the key that opens heaven's gate. Just as we need passports when entering a sovereign land, we need the certificate that reads "cleansed by the blood of the crucified Lord" to enter heaven.

In God's justice sin must be punished, but because of God's great love for us, He provided a way for our sins to be pardoned. The Bible tells us, "For God so loved the world that he gave his one and only Son, that whoever believes in him shall not perish but have eternal life" (John 3:16 NIV).

Karl Barth, the noted Swiss theologian, was among the greatest Christian thinkers of the twentieth century. Pope Pius XII described him as the most important theologian since Thomas Aquinas. It is said that at the conclusion of one of his lectures he was asked, "Dr. Barth, what do you consider to be the most profound theological concept that has captivated your mind?"

Forgiveness: The Key to Heaven

All the audience members had their pencils poised, ready for some deep theological concept. Imagine their surprise when he replied without hesitation, "Jesus loves me, this I know, for the Bible tells me so."

Sam Hadley of the Water Street Mission in New York told about the most memorable event in his long association with the mission:

> An old drunk, called the Major, came into the mission one night just at closing and started down the aisle toward the kneeling bench. He knew it was our custom to give a bowl of hot soup and a warm bed to anyone who came to pray at the last service. The old Major took advantage of this policy as often as he dared.
>
> Mr. Hadley saw him approaching, and he said, "I was tired and irritated, so I did something I had never done before and would never do again. I met him halfway, turned him around, and gave him the bum's rush out the front door.
>
> "That night I couldn't sleep, so I got up from my bed, put on my clothes, and started out to find the Major. I didn't have to look very far. I found him lying on the back porch of a nearby bar, fast asleep.
>
> "As I looked into his bearded face I saw something I had never noticed before. It must have been the same thing that Jesus saw when he looked into the face of Simon Peter, Andrew, Levi, or any number of men who came in contact with Jesus. I sat down on the step beside him and put his head on my lap. I said, 'Major, I'm sorry for what I did, I love you and Jesus loves you. I want you to come back to the Mission and have a bowl of hot soup and a warm bed.'
>
> "He sat bolt upright and asked, 'What did you say, Hadley?'
>
> "I repeated, 'I want you to have a bowl of hot soup and a warm bed.'
>
> "'No, what did you say before that?'

Forgiveness: The Key to Lasting Joy

"So I repeated, 'I love you and Jesus loves you.'

"At this he broke down in tears and sobbed, 'That's the first time anyone has used that word for me ever since my daughter was killed and I turned to drink.'

"The old Major was a transformed man from that time on. He lived only six months, but during that time God used him to straighten out the lives of dozens of men."

It is Jesus' love as found in the Bible that brings transformation into hearts and lives broken by sin.

It is understandable that many preachers prefer to talk about God's love rather than God's wrath and the subject of hell; however, when Jonathan Edwards, during the eighteenth century's Great Awakening, preached a famous sermon called *Sinners in the Hands of an Angry God*, multitudes of people repented of their sins and came to Christ to escape hell.

The same Bible that tells us about heaven also tells us there is a hell. God assures us that He doesn't want us to go there. "The Lord is … not willing that any should perish, but that all should come to repentance" (2 Peter 3:9 KJV). Jesus lets us know that hell was not prepared for people: "Then I will turn to those on my left and say, 'Away with you, you cursed ones, into the eternal fire prepared for the devil and his demons'" (Matt. 25:41 TLB).

The wonderful news is that God provides a way for us to escape the punishment we deserve for our sins. He rescues us from hell's agony and opens before us the path to heaven's ecstasy. God's plan was to allow His perfect Son, Jesus Christ, to take on Himself the punishment for our sin. The Scripture declares, "Christ also suffered. He died once for the sins of all us guilty sinners although he himself was innocent of any sin at any time, that he might bring us safely home to God" (1 Peter 3:18 TLB).

Forgiveness: The Key to Heaven

Some people can't bring themselves to admit that they are sinners. They try to justify their behavior by comparing themselves with other sinners, but the issue is how they look to our holy, sinless God. Even our best efforts and our most righteous deeds look like filthy rags to Him. The Bible says, "All have sinned and fall short of the glory of God" (Rom. 3:23).

The Bible tells us that sin pays wages. "For the wages of sin is death, but the gift of God is eternal life in Christ Jesus our Lord" (Rom. 6:23). Aren't you glad God provided the perfect substitute to take the punishment for our sins? He freely gives us the greatest gift He could give—forgiveness and eternal life—when we place our faith and trust in His Son, Jesus Christ.

Some people think they can gain heaven and eternal life by being good or by giving to charity. That would be like trying to pay God for His great and priceless gift. If heaven isn't ours as a free gift, it isn't ours at all. We need to receive the gift and thank the Giver.

The Bible says: "For if you tell others with your own mouth that Jesus Christ is your Lord and believe in your own heart that God has raised him from the dead, you will be saved. For it is by believing in his heart that a man becomes right with God; and with his mouth he tells others of his faith, confirming his salvation" (Rom. 10:9–10 TLB).

I boarded the train at Denver's Union Station and made my way through the coach to find an empty seat. I prayed that the Lord would lead me to a person with whom I could share His love. Then I spotted him—Methuselah.

I introduced myself and met Mr. Roger Chapin of Harrow, Ontario, Canada. The other passengers met us too. They couldn't help themselves because my seatmate was very hard of hearing. Mr. Chapin was on his way to Las Vegas. He had just turned eighty-nine, and he had been a widower for two years.

"Lunch is now being served in the dining car," the loudspeaker crackled.

Forgiveness: The Key to Lasting Joy

I repeated the message to my companion. When he stood to go to lunch, he was my stereotype of a refined Canadian gentleman dressed in his sweater vest and tweed suit.

We returned to our seats after eating lunch together, and my aged friend fell asleep. I read my Bible. Mr. Chapin began to stir and he looked over at me.

"Do you read the Bible?" I asked.

"No, but my wife used to. She was the religious one in our family."

I read and quoted some of my favorite verses to him. Looking about, I noticed people listening—especially one lady who nodded in agreement and encouragement. I was certain she was praying for Mr. Chapin and for me.

I recounted my own story of how I came to know the Lord when I was a teenager, asking Christ to forgive my sins and come into my heart.

Mr. Chapin said, "Well, I guess it's OK for you and my wife, but I never believed all that, and I'm too old to change now."

It was late at night and the train whistled over the tracks while the passengers slept.

"How did you say I could become a Christian?" Mr. Chapin's question reverberated throughout the car.

I quoted from the Bible, "Believe on the Lord Jesus Christ and you will be saved. If you confess with your mouth, Jesus as Lord, and believe in your heart that God raised Jesus from the dead, you will be saved." I added, "Pray and ask Jesus to forgive your sins and come into your heart."

It struck me funny that because Mr. Chapin was so hard of hearing, God not only helped me share His Word with my seat companion, but also with the other passengers throughout our coach.

When first light appeared, I looked at Mr. Chapin, half expecting him to be glowing like an angel. He looked the same or perhaps a little older and more tired. We would part soon, and I wanted so much to hear him say that he had become a Christian.

Forgiveness: The Key to Heaven

Finally I got up courage to ask, "Did you invite Jesus to come into your heart?"

"No," he said, "I'm just not ready to do that."

Over the loudspeaker came the conductor's voice: "Las Vegas, next stop in ten minutes. If Las Vegas is your destination, gather up your belongings."

We stood on the platform as Mr. Chapin took my hand and held it. I gave him a tentative hug, not knowing if Canadian gentlemen hugged. He turned and left, looking old, stooped, and lonely. He hadn't become a Christian.

"Oh, God," I prayed, "give him another opportunity to come to You."

I wrote to Mr. Chapin and he answered. As the months passed and holidays came, I sent him cards for Thanksgiving, Christmas, and Easter. A little plan began to form in my mind. We were to attend a convention in Milwaukee in June. I wondered how far that was from Harrow, Canada, and if we could visit Mr. Chapin after the convention.

My little plan worked out and Mr. Chapin welcomed us cordially into his home. We enjoyed seeing photographs of Mr. Chapin and his wife—especially their wedding pictures. He asked us to walk with him to the small cemetery across the road.

"I come here often," he said as we stopped at the headstone of his wife's grave. "This is my plot beside her."

Back in his living room, I realized it was time for us to leave. There was urgency, almost panic, in my prayer as I asked God for one last opportunity to invite Mr. Chapin to receive the Lord. I picked up their wedding picture.

Roland said, "Roger, remember when you married your sweetheart you were asked, 'Roger, do you take this woman as your wife?' You responded, 'I do,' and your married life began. The Christian life begins when you say, 'I do' to the Lord. Would you like to do that right now?"

Mr. Chapin nodded his head, and using those exact words he said, "I do to the Lord."

Forgiveness: The Key to Lasting Joy

That was the last time I saw Roger Chapin. I wrote to him and sent devotional literature. I received one letter after our visit, but then there was no response—no "return to sender," no deceased notice, nothing. I tried to call him, but his phone was no longer in service.

I don't know how long Roger Chapin lived after he said, "I do to the Lord." I do know God has promised a place in heaven for Roger and his wife and for everyone who says, "I do to the Lord."

As a pastor and wife, we have had hundreds of opportunities to talk to people about their relationship with Jesus Christ. It has been our privilege and responsibility to tell others about the most important Person in our lives. The truth is that it is every Christian's responsibility to share with others what Christ means to them. We know the cure for the deadly cancer of sin. How selfish we would be if we didn't share that life-giving cure with people who are without hope.

The late D. James Kennedy in his book *Evangelism Explosion* suggests a good question to help determine a person's understanding of the Christian faith: "Have you come to a place in your spiritual life where you know for certain that if you were to die today you would go to heaven?"

The answer that comes from many people is, "I guess so, I hope so, but I don't think anyone can know for sure."

How sad it would be if we had to go through life without the assurance of God's forgiveness and a place in heaven. We indeed can be sure we will go to heaven. The Bible says, "These things I have written to you who believe in the name of the Son of God, so that you may know that you have eternal life" (1 John 5:13 NASB).

I'm a fixer, but I can't fix things because I'm not mechanically inclined. Our son Jim is also a fixer, but he can fix almost everything

Forgiveness: The Key to Heaven

because he has a mechanical engineer's mind. His talent is greatly appreciated. His daughter Kylie recently said to me, "Grandma, Dad has really set the bar high. I'm going to have a hard time finding a husband who can live up to his abilities."

When our granddaughter Jaclyn broke one of her toys, she said, "It's OK, Daddy can fix it. Daddy can fix anything."

Since I can't fix things, I guess it's logical that I'm obsessed with a desire to fix people. No one appreciates a people fixer, though. In fact, I guess I sometimes deserve the title "busybody." The truth is I certainly realize I can't fix anybody, but I know who can: Jesus. The Bible tells us how broken people (we are all broken by sin) can have new life and wholeness in Christ.

We can't fix ourselves no matter how hard we try. Our family, our friends, and our psychiatrist can't fix us. We need to have our sins forgiven and begin again. We can't fix the old self because we are beyond repair. We need new life in Christ. Scripture assures us, "When someone becomes a Christian, he becomes a brand new person inside. He is not the same anymore. A new life has begun!" (2 Cor. 5:17 TLB).

I want to help people come to know Christ as their Savior. I also want to help them fix their broken relationships. I've seen the sadness resulting from fractured relationships within marriage, the family, and the church. I've also seen how good and pleasant life can be when people live together in harmony. Jesus said in the Sermon on the Mount, "Blessed are the peacemakers: for they shall be called the children of God" (Matt. 5:9 KJV). I really do long to be the kind of fixer who is a peacemaker.

I tried to be a matchmaker once or twice, but without success. I'd rather be a peacemaker anyway.

God is the fixer. He fixes broken people and broken relationships. He made us, so only He knows what makes us tick. His Word is the instruction manual—if we study it, ask for His enlightenment, and follow the directions He gives, we will be made new.

Most of us are eager to talk about the most important people in our lives—our spouses, our children, and especially our grandchildren. Sports enthusiasts are great talkers when it comes to a

Forgiveness: The Key to Lasting Joy

discussion of their favorite athletes. In the same way, Christians should be delighted to tell others about their relationship with Jesus Christ, the one who has given them new life and hope for eternity.

Dr. Lyman Abbott, a theologian whose books received wide acclaim, was asked to review his volume titled *What Christianity Means to Me*. It was fifteen minutes before the service was scheduled to begin, and already the huge church was filled to standing room only. As the author waited in the church study, the pastor entered, handed him a copy of his book, and said, "Please sign it and write the ripest thought that has come to you during the sixty years of your ministry." Then he left to allow Abbott some time to think.

When the pastor returned, he read the page where the author had written: "Christianity is not a philosophy that Jesus came to teach, it is a life that Jesus came to impart."

The apostle Paul recognized that he was a recipient of that life Christ came to impart. He wrote, "For to me to live is Christ" (Phil. 1:21 KJV).

When we think God wants us to tell someone about the new life Jesus has imparted to us, it is natural to feel inadequate. The subject is of such importance that we want to say just the right thing to help that person come to know the Lord.

The best way to share our faith is to tell the story of our own conversion. Regardless of whether it was a dramatic event or a quiet transfer of authority from the kingdom of self to the kingdom of Christ, God can use our personal experience to impact the lives of those who hear it.

C. S. Lewis, one of the world's most celebrated thinkers and authors, was asked to tell how he moved from atheism to Christianity, which he did in his autobiographical conversion story, *Surprised by Joy*. He tells how many of the scholars and writers he most admired turned out to be Christians. God used notable individuals such as McDonald, Chesterton, Tolkien, and Herbert to impact Lewis's thinking. There were many other Christians whose writing and friendship exerted a great deal of influence in bringing him to faith.

Forgiveness: The Key to Heaven

C. S. Lewis's scholarly writings in books such as *Mere Christianity* stretch the minds of most theologians, but he also was able to simplify the message of God's redemptive plan in his classic series The Chronicles of Narnia, which is loved and understood by children and adults. These books help us understand how the great Creator became our Savior.

God used the words of some great scholars to bring C. S. Lewis to Himself, but He also uses the stumbling words of any Christian who is willing to share his faith. There's a wise saying, "A word fitly spoken is like apples of gold in settings of silver" (Prov. 25:11). Sometimes those words fitly spoken might come from a Christian nurse attending a patient in the hospital or from a passenger to a seat companion on a train or airplane. God's Spirit can use appropriate words to help an individual come to the point of decision for Christ. Usually there is someone in that person's life who has already planted the seed of God's Word and has been praying for that individual too. Perhaps God will give you just the right words needed at the right time to bring new life to that someone near you.

Jesus came to save the lost. To illustrate this, the master storyteller told four parables about the lost. He told the story of a sheep that was lost, but was found and brought rejoicing to the shepherd. He told about a valuable coin that was lost, but was found and brought rejoicing to the owner. He told about a boy who went into the far country and was lost until he came to himself and then to his father, and there was rejoicing because he was found. Then Jesus told about the lost elder brother whose self-righteousness kept him from fellowship with his father. This story ends in sadness, because there is no record of this brother being found.

Jesus tells us that there is joy in heaven over one sinner who repents. The amazing record of the repentant thief on the cross (Luke 23) tells us the extent to which our Lord will go in granting pardon to anyone who asks Him for forgiveness.

Forgiveness: The Key to Lasting Joy

Two criminals were led out to be executed with Jesus. God's Son was nailed to the center cross and the criminals were crucified on the right and left of Him.

The crowd watched and ridiculed. The Jewish leaders laughed and railed against Jesus. The soldiers mocked. Jesus prayed, "Father, forgive these people, for they know not what they are doing."

At first the two thieves joined the others in their abusive language. One of them scoffed, "So you're the Messiah, are you? Prove it by saving yourself and us while you're at it!"

The other criminal protested, "Don't you even fear God when you're dying? We deserve to die for our evil deeds, but this man hasn't done one thing wrong." Then he said, "Jesus, remember me when You come into Your kingdom."

Jesus replied, "Today you'll be with Me in paradise. This is a solemn promise."

Forgiveness was the key to heaven for this guilty sinner. The thief on the cross didn't have time to earn his way to heaven by his good works. He could not use his ill-gained wealth to pay his entrance fee, and he did not have time to make atonement for his misspent youth. He relied totally on God's mercy, and his sins were freely forgiven.

In her well known hymn "Wonderful, Wonderful Jesus," Anna B. Russell wrote: "There is never a guilty sinner, there is never a wand'ring one but that God can in mercy pardon, through Jesus Christ, His Son."

The Bible backs this up by stating, "[Jesus] is able to save completely all who come to God through him. Since he will live forever, he will always be there [in heaven] to remind God that he has paid for their sins with his blood" (Heb. 7:25 TLB).

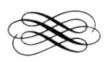

When Roland and I visited Westminster Abbey we were reminded of a traveler in Europe who had an interesting story to tell. He said that a little old lady was a member of their tour group.

Forgiveness: *The Key to Heaven*

Her clothes always looked like they'd been packed too tightly in her suitcase, but there was no one more alert than she.

This lady always stayed as close as possible to the tour guide so she wouldn't miss anything. When they went to Westminster Abbey, she read aloud the words on the pulpit, "We have an Advocate with the Father, Jesus Christ the righteous."

They listened to the guide as he pointed to some of the monuments that were erected in memory of England's illustrious dead. He showed them the seats where the kings and queens had sat. And then he concluded his tour by stating somewhat arrogantly, "This is the most famous church in all the world" and asking if there were any questions.

Up went the little old lady's hand. "Yes, I have a question. Has anybody been saved here recently?"

The guide seemed confused, and after a few moments he said, "I don't understand your question. Would you please repeat it?"

In a voice that could be heard echoing throughout the abbey, she repeated, "Has anybody been saved here recently?"

The guide was silent for several moments before he responded, "I'm afraid I don't have an answer. I've never been asked that question before."

The tourist told us, "I'm a traveling salesman, so I attend many different church services. Whenever I get settled in a church pew, I hear that little old lady's question in my head: 'Has anybody been saved here recently?'"

The purpose of our Lord in coming to the earth was not to build great cathedrals or impressive church buildings. Jesus Himself told us: "The Son of Man has come to seek and to save that which was lost" (Luke 19:10).

We were privileged to share some time with a young Chinese girl when she was on a summer project in the United States. She is currently enrolled in graduate studies in Germany and we have

Forgiveness: The Key to Lasting Joy

kept in touch. She sent us an e-mail asking us to tell her how we celebrate Easter. She wrote, "Would you mind sharing a little bit with me? I'm very interested."

Of course we were delighted to tell our young friend, who grew up as an atheist in Communist China, about the meaning of Easter. We wrote:

> In answer to your question about Easter—the foundation of the Christian faith is the life, death, and resurrection of Jesus Christ. He lived a righteous and perfect life that we, because of our fallen and corrupt nature, cannot. He was beaten and nailed to a cross where He suffered the penalty for our sins. While He was suffering for the sins of the whole world, He prayed, "Father forgive them for they know not what they do." He took our guilt upon Himself and died the horrible death of crucifixion.
>
> He was placed in a tomb, but He rose bodily from the dead that first Easter morning. The early Christians were so happy when they first learned that Christ was alive and well that they greeted each other with, "The Lord is risen!" The response was, "He is risen indeed!" We continue to greet one another with that same greeting and response today. Christ gave His life for our sins, yours and mine, and was buried. The message of Easter is that Jesus rose from the dead. Because Jesus lives, all those who believe in Him and receive God's forgiveness will also live with Him in Heaven forever. Happy Easter!

We continue to pray that our young Chinese friend will come to faith in Christ.

There's a short but powerful prayer in 1 Chronicles. In the last part of his earnest prayer, Jabez prays, "Oh, that You would bless me indeed, and enlarge my territory, that Your hand would be with me, and that You would keep me from evil, that I may not cause pain!" (1 Chron. 4:10).

Forgiveness: The Key to Heaven

I often pray this prayer, especially the last part. I ask that God will keep me from evil that I will not cause pain or reproach on the name of Christ. I became a Christian when I was thirteen and I have been an outspoken follower of Christ ever since. Yet I have many family members and friends who have not yet committed their lives to Christ, and I don't want my actions or words to be a hindrance that keeps them from the Lord. I've never claimed to be more than a forgiven sinner, but somehow Christians can be labeled as self-righteous or hypocritical. The truth is, Christians know we aren't perfect and that our own righteousness is nothing in God's sight. We know we could never do enough good deeds to purchase our entrance into heaven, so we cast ourselves on the mercy of God's forgiveness through Christ.

It is our prayer that our lives will be a light that will draw people to Christ. We know that as much as we want to see our friends and family members come to the Lord, we can't, by our own efforts and desire, bring anyone to God. We can pray, tell our own story of conversion, and try to live the Christian life, but it is God, through the work of the Holy Spirit, who convicts people of sin and draws them to Christ. Jesus said, "Truly, truly, I say to you, he who hears My word, and believes Him who sent Me, has eternal life, and does not come into judgment, but has passed out of death into life" (John 5:24 NASB).

Forgiveness is a choice. Each person must choose for himself: eternal life or eternal death. Receiving God's forgiveness is up to us. He has done all that is required in His justice and mercy to offer us forgiveness and life eternal in heaven. Accepting His forgiveness is an act of our will.

Missionaries have gone to the most remote regions of the earth to tell people of every race that God offers His forgiveness to the whole world. There are countless stories of those who, down through the centuries, have risked their lives to take the gospel to distant lands. Bible translators have worked for years to reduce the language of a single tribe into a written form and then translate the Bible into that language. The American Bible Society and other Christian groups have distributed the Bible in hundreds of different languages.

Forgiveness: The Key to Lasting Joy

Their motivation for doing this is the sincere conviction that personal salvation is a matter of life or death, of heaven or hell. The Bible says, "Faith comes by hearing, and hearing by the word of God" (Rom. 10:17). Christians, in obedience to God and in their desire to see people receive God's forgiveness, have taken the good news of the gospel throughout the world.

Many Christians who have not been able to go as missionaries to distant parts of the world have faithfully prayed for the spread of God's message of love and forgiveness. We know that prayer is of great importance in bringing people to know Christ at home and abroad. We pray for those we don't even know to come to Christ, and it is our special privilege and responsibility to pray for members of our own family to come to know Him.

My mother and I prayed many times together for specific family members who were not yet Christians. On one memorable occasion the two of us were seated on a bench as we watched a full moon rise over the Sea of Galilee. We prayed there together for my mother's children and grandchildren to come to Christ. God answered that prayer when several of them received the Lord at her funeral. God is continuing to answer her prayers today, many years after she has gone to heaven.

The words *I love you* are beautiful to hear. I remember how thrilled I was when I said, "I love you" to my grandchildren and they answered just the way I wanted. First Kylie, then Cody, Cassidy, Taylor, and Jaclyn responded, "I love you too, Grandma."

When our sixth grandchild, Sarah, arrived from Uganda, we couldn't wait to lavish our love and affection on her. She seemed to welcome our hugs and expressions of endearment, but when I said, "I love you, Sarah," she was silent. It was a red-letter-day for me when she first said, "I love you too, Grandma." I was moved to tears.

Forgiveness: The Key to Heaven

That day I sat down and wrote my thoughts on how God has demonstrated His love for us and has waited for us to respond. How it must please Him when at last He hears us say, "I love You too, God." For some of us He waited a long time, but He never gave up on us.

Since that first time Sarah said, "I love you too, Grandma," she has said it over and over again. It brings a smile to my face and a lift to my heart every time I hear it. When Sarah came to understand how much I love her, she came to love me.

God shows His love for us every day. When we see His creation and read His Word, He says to us, "I love you." The Bible says, "We love him because he first loved us" (1 John 4:19 KJV). The greatest expression of God's love is found in His gift of forgiveness and eternal life in heaven through Jesus Christ, His Son. When we accept that forgiveness, we can say in response to His amazing love, "I love You too, God."

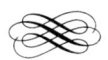

Life, now and eternal, is all about forgiveness. We are admonished in the Bible to accept God's forgiveness through Christ and to forgive others.

The key to happiness in marriage and in the family is forgiveness. The path to healing after suffering the pain of tragedy is forgiveness. The unity of churches after disagreements is dependent on forgiveness. We are welcomed into heaven because of God's forgiveness of our sins through Jesus Christ our Lord.

Yes, life, now and eternal, is all about forgiveness.

Your Turn

1. Why do you think some people refuse to accept God's forgiveness? Do these people intend to reject God's forgiveness or do they think they can postpone a decision?

Forgiveness: The Key to Lasting Joy

2. How do you deal with doubts? Do you have the assurance of sins forgiven and a home in heaven? If not, please see the next section for how you can experience God's forgiveness.

3. What led you to your decision to commit your life to Jesus Christ? How can you share your faith with others?

How You Can Experience God's Forgiveness

Repent:
    To repent means that you recognize that you are a sinner. You tell God you are sorry for your sins and ask for His forgiveness. "For all have sinned and fall short of the glory of God."
    —Romans 3:23

Believe:
    To become a Christian, you need to believe that Jesus died on the cross and rose from the dead. "Christ died for our sins ... He was buried ... He rose again."
    —1 Corinthians 15:3–4

Receive:
    To receive God's free gift of forgiveness and eternal life, invite Jesus Christ to come into your life. "As many as received Him, to them He gave the right to become children of God."
    —John 1:12

Pray:
    If you pray the following simple prayer with sincerity, you can know you are born into God's family:

Forgiveness: The Key to Lasting Joy

Dear Jesus, I know I am a sinner and I need Your forgiveness. I believe You died on the cross and rose from the dead. I want to turn from my sin and follow You. I now invite You to be my Lord and Savior. Thank You for Your gift of eternal life. In Jesus' name, Amen.

About the Authors

ROLAND SPENT PART of his childhood in Colombia, South America, where his parents were missionaries. After his father's death, his family returned to Southern California. He received his education at Culter Academy, The Bible Institute of Los Angeles, and California Baptist Seminary. He traveled extensively as a soloist and as a member of a boys' quartet.

Gayle was born in Twentynine Palms, California, where she attended school and worked at her parents' soda fountain. After college she returned to her childhood home for a time to manage the family business. It was there that she met a young minister who was completing his final year of seminary while preaching and teaching in a local church. They were married in The Little Church of the Desert.

Roland served two churches in Southern California before he was called to Denver, Colorado, where he served as senior pastor of Crossroads Baptist Church for twenty-nine years. He enjoyed an interim pastorate in Grand Junction, which rounded out thirty years of ministry in Colorado. He is the author of two books: *Patriarchs in Poetry, Genesis*, and *Harmony of the Gospels in Rhyming Verse*.

In addition to her role as homemaker and pastor's wife, Gayle taught elementary school in Colorado for twenty-four years.

Forgiveness: The Key to Lasting Joy

Roland and Gayle have been married fifty-five years. They have two sons, who have lovely wives, and a daughter who has a great husband. They are the proud grandparents of one grandson and five granddaughters. They also are happy to claim nine grandchildren sponsored by members of the family through Compassion International.

Notes

p. 13 Bill Morelan, *Married for Life: Secrets from those Married 50 years or More* (Colorado Springs, CO: David C. Cook, 2004).

p. 16 Harold Arlen and Johnny Mercer, *Ac-Cent-Tchu-Ate the Positive*, 1944.

p. 24 C. Roy Angell, *Shields of Brass* (Nashville, TN: Broadman Press, 1965), 99.

p. 29 Roland S. Taylor, *Harmony of the Gospels in Rhyming Verse* (Bloomington, IN: Authorhouse, 2002), 233.

p. 38 Dwight David Eisenhower, *At Ease: Stories I Tell to Friends* (Garden City, NY: Doubleday, 1967).

p. 42 *Father's Song*, Steve Taylor, C. A. Music, 1982.

p. 44 C. Maude Battersby, *An Evening Prayer*, public domain (circa 1895).

p. 44 My recollection is that this story is attributed to Edmund Burke, but I'm unable to provide independent verification.

p. 76 Oswald J. Smith and B. D. Ackley, *God Understands*, Word Music LLC, 1937.

p. 79 Viktor E. Frankl, *Man's Search for Meaning* (Austria: Verlag fur Jugend und Volk, 1946/Boston, MA: Beacon Press, 1959, 1962, 1984).

Forgiveness: The Key to Lasting Joy

p. 81 Carol Ragan, *Carol's Kitchen Brochure.*

p. 81 Amy Biehl, Wikipedia, *Peacemaker Hero: Amy Biehl.*

p. 83 Corrie ten Boom, *Tramp for the Lord* (Fort Washington, PA: Jove Books/Penguin/CLC Publications, 1986).

p. 84 Paul Lee Tan, *Encyclopedia of 7700 Illustrations* (Rockville, MD: Assurance Publishers, 1979), "Saved By His Worst Enemy," # 1768.

p. 99 C. Roy Angell, *Iron Shoes* (Nashville, TN: Broadman Press, 1953), 60.

p. 104 D. James Kennedy, *Evangelism Explosion* (Wheaton, IL: Tyndale House Publishers, 1970).

p. 109 C. Roy Angell, *Shields of Brass* (Nashville, TN: Broadman Press 1965), 15.

WinePressPublishing
Great Books, Defined.

To order additional copies of this book call:
1-877-421-READ (7323)
or please visit our website at
www.WinePressbooks.com

If you enjoyed this quality custom-published book,
drop by our website for more books and information.

www.winepresspublishing.com
"Your partner in custom publishing."